Dancing in Moonlight:

Understanding Artemis Through Celebration

Thista Minai

Dancing In Moonlight

Understanding Artemis Through Celebration

Thista Minai

Hubbardston, Massachusetts

Asphodel Press
12 Simond Hill Road
Hubbardston, MA 01452

Dancing In Moonlight

ISBN: 978-0-6151-8818-8

Printed in cooperation with
Lulu Enterprises, Inc.
860 Aviation Parkway, Suite 300
Morrisville, NC 27560

For Artemis

Thanks to my family for accepting me as I am.

Contents

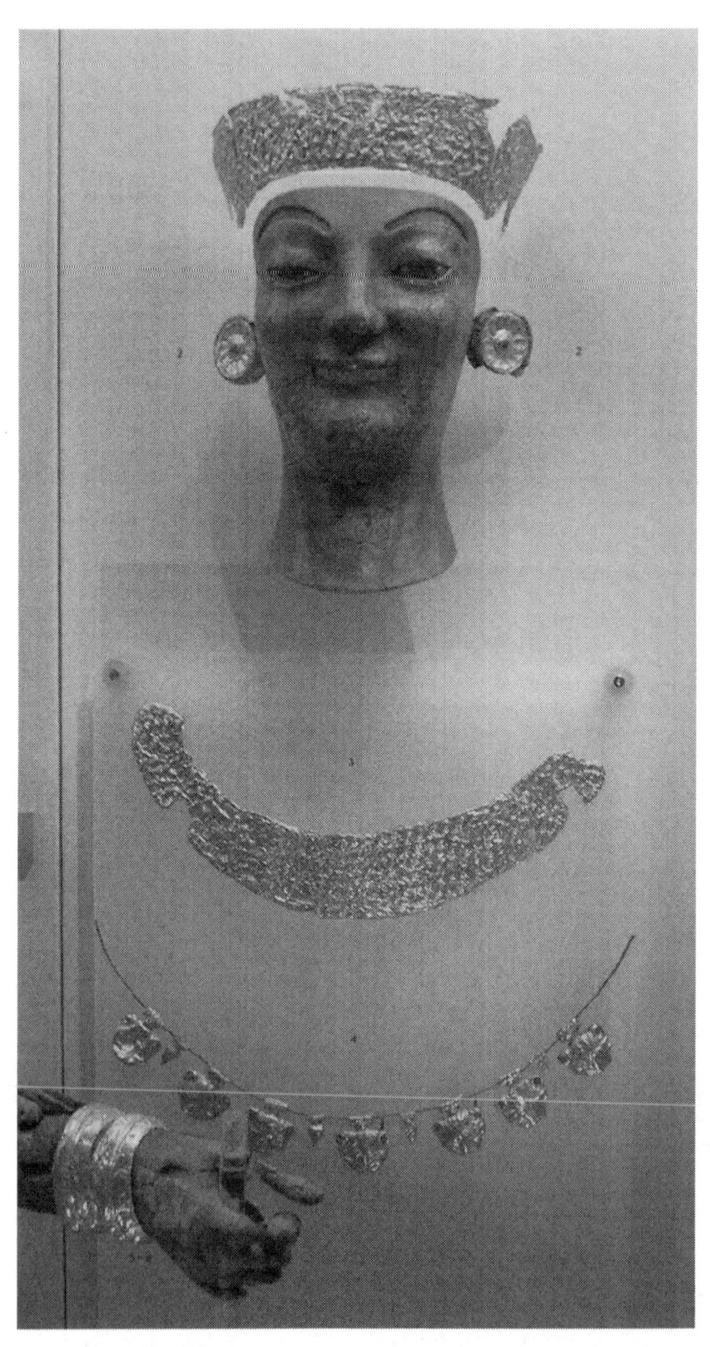

The remains of an elephantine and gold image of Artemis wearing a necklace of golden lion heads. (Archaeological Museum of Delphi)

Introduction

New Hellenic Religion

Artemis is an ancient Goddess with more aspects and manifestations than any single book could hope to cover. There is plenty of information about Her waiting out there for the apt student to discover it, but the sheer volume of that information can be somewhat intimidating; perhaps even a life's work could not unveil its entirety. While researching the ancient world and Artemis's manifestations within it is an invaluable aid to understanding Her and Her nature, this can only carry one so far. Part of discovering Artemis must come by actually approaching Her.

This book is designed for people who want to get to know Artemis through action and personal experience. In it I describe six modern festivals held in honor of Artemis, and two joint festivals She shares with other Gods. This book explains where these festivals come from, how you can put them on for your own community, and what you might get out of them.

Just about everyone has at least heard of Greek mythology, as most schools teach or at least offer courses in the basics of Greek myth and lore. Even those who feel no inclination towards ancient Greek religion can still acknowledge the fact that the ancient Greek civilizations had an immense impact on the modern western world. For some of us, however, the ancient Greek Gods are more than just fictional characters or archetypal figures. They are still very much alive (as one would expect of immortals), and They can still bless our lives with Their divine gifts.

There are many different equally valid ways to honor the Greek Gods. Many types of modern Neo-Paganism allow for some incorporation of ancient Greek elements or entities. *Hellenismos*, a term used by the Roman emperor Julian (among others) to describe the religion and customs of the ancient Greeks, is now used by many modern people to describe a path of Greek reconstructionism. People who practice Hellenismos, some of whom refer to themselves as *Hellenistai*[1], attempt to recreate the religion and customs of ancient Greece while putting them into the context of the modern world. Scholarly research on ancient practices is mixed with inspiration and modern invention to create the new Hellenic religion that is called Hellenismos today.

Honestly, I don't think Artemis cares if we honor Her as the ancient Greeks did or not. I would guess that Hellenismos or Hellenic ritual is like home to the ancient Greek Gods; They feel most comfortable and relaxed with it. However, They can easily be pleased by other types of rituals, just as people can be pleased by vacations to new and different places. Perhaps there are some other traditions or styles of worship the ancient Greek Gods like a whole lot, in the same way that some people have locations they visit over and over. Nevertheless, I think that Hellenismos is home to Them, and thus They will always feel most comfortable with that type of worship. Of course, that doesn't mean They would be any less honored by any other type of worship. I think that the effort of reconstructing ancient Greek rituals for Artemis is an honorable offering, but She would be equally pleased by any form of worship that requires the same amount of thought and effort.

That said, there are some tremendous benefits to studying ancient Greek religion and practicing reconstructionism. Learning about how Artemis manifested in ancient Greece can help us understand Her. We come to understand the underlying essence of Who and What She is beneath the cultural trappings of any age precisely because we have to struggle to comprehend the meaning of Her various myths and rituals within an ancient Greek context. Translation requires a solid grasp of meaning. Such studies can keep us honest, and can ensure that we do not make up supposed manifestations and myths of Artemis purely to suit our own motives. Discovering Artemis as the ancient Greeks knew Her can also remind us that we're not crazy, that people three thousand years ago had some of the same experiences with the same being we know now. We may see Her in different clothes (perhaps figuratively, perhaps literally), but She's still the same Goddess, and it can be inspiring and empowering to realize how long people have shared these similar experiences with Her.

Since I am a self-proclaimed Helleniste, this book will inevitably approach Artemis from a reconstructionist point of view. While the festivals I will present are Hellenic rituals, one need not be a Helleniste to celebrate them. My hope is that anyone at all who wishes to discover Artemis or to create a deeper connection with Her can use these festivals to learn about Her and to establish or embellish their own relationship with Her. For readers interested in Hellenismos as a spiritual path, I recommend *Greek Religion* by Walter Burkert for more information on ancient Greek religion, and *Kharis: Hellenic Polytheism Explored* by Sarah Kate Istra Winter for more information on modern Hellenismos.

Many Neo-Pagans like to say that the Gods change over time. I heartily disagree. I believe that the Gods Themselves do not change, but the way that They manifest to humans most certainly does. A modern person might experience Artemis, for example, wearing camouflage, wielding a sniper rifle and choosing to sleep with whomever She will, and thus say that Artemis has changed. I would say that such an experience shows quite clearly that Artemis has not changed, that She has, in fact, stayed exactly the same. Artemis as the ultimate efficient huntress with absolute freedom might manifest to an ancient Greek as a bow-wielding virgin, but to a modern woman, perhaps the independent sniper better conveys that same essence. As far as I can tell, the Gods are what They have always been and what They always will be, but the way that we see and interact with them can change with our cultural context.

I have my opinions about Who and What Artemis is and is not. That does not necessarily invalidate the opinions of others, and I do not claim to know the "One True Way" of honoring Artemis. Maybe She has some reason for wanting us to see Her in different ways; maybe it's not a matter of wrong or right, but rather of the right person hearing the right things. Maybe each person needs to approach Her or come to Her in the way that is right for them, and no single individual can provide that for everyone. Nevertheless, I have developed my own opinions on Who She is based on my experiences with Her, and that does include some thoughts about other people being right or wrong. After all, polytheism does not mean that the Gods are whatever we imagine Them to be; it means anything we can imagine has a God of it. That said, I know that I am only human, and I could be wrong.

I would rather people argue with me than just blindly accept what I say. If you disagree with my opinions, that means you are actively thinking about your own ideas and formulating your own point of view. I feel that is far better than mindless regurgitation of the words of any author. I am just as entitled to my opinions as anyone is entitled to theirs, and I openly encourage discussion and debate that helps us all reexamine and redevelop our own ideas.

I can't pretend to know the true nature of the Gods. I think I would burn up just like Semele if They ever tried to reveal it to me. All I do know is what They show me. It's clear that many people see Artemis in different ways. Maybe some of us are wrong. Maybe all of us are right. All that I know for sure is what She shows me, what I experience with Her. What She is to me, how I know Her, what She whispers to me... I believe that these are the things I need to carry across into the rest of the world and show to other people who want to see them. Perhaps the reason there are so many of us with so many different interpretations of Her is that She Herself is too huge for any one person to convey completely.

Festivals

This book is about festivals that honor Artemis. The word "festival" is not, in this context, interchangeable with the word ritual. A Hellenic festival contains many activities, only some of which will be rites or rituals. A festival is meant to be a celebration. The Gods are honored not only with offerings and rituals, but also with a myriad of activities that enhance the occasion. Each of these activities provides an opportunity for participants to draw closer to divinity through action, and all of these elements together comprise what we call a festival.

Cataleos

The Temple of Artemis at Cataleos is a semi-public sacred space dedicated to Artemis, currently located in Cambridge, Massachusetts. More information about the temple itself can be found at http://www.cataleos.org. It bears mentioning here only because the festivals I present in this book were originally intended to be public or semi-public celebrations held in the Cataleos temple space. They were designed to be suitable to the environment at Cataleos, and include rites and customs that have become a tradition there. Other groups or temples most certainly have their own ways of holding festivals, and many have their own festivals as well. The celebrations I describe here are not the only correct way to observe these particular festivals; this is simply the way we do them at Cataleos.

I must pause here and define the terms "public" and "semi-public". A truly public festival is open to any random person who decides they want to attend. Anyone who happens to hear of the festival is welcome to show up and join in the celebration. A semi-public celebration is open to anyone, but they must confer with the individual in charge beforehand. I have discovered over time that certain occasions can be appropriate for a truly random group of whoever happens to come along, while others require more discretion. When a festival is held largely in someone's home, it is important to be sure that everyone attending will deal respectfully with their host and their surroundings. In a public setting such as a park or a community center, this can be less of an issue. In some situations it's especially important to make sure that every participant feels they are in a safe environment. In these cases you may find that certain individuals do not work well with everyone else, and you may need to limit who can attend your celebration. In a truly public festival, you must be ready to deal with distracting or destructive elements that might arise; you never know who might come or what they might do, so you must be ready for anything.

The Cataleos festivals can be presented as public, semi-public or private celebrations. While they were initially designed to be public occasions, they can be (and have been) easily adapted to more selective or even strictly private groups. If you decide to hold your own Cataleos-style celebrations, I strongly recommend you think very seriously on what type of group you wish to present your festivals to. If you attempt a truly public festival, be sure that you are properly prepared. If you are creating a festival for a private group with a consistent membership, then perhaps you will want to adapt certain elements to make them particularly applicable to you and your groups.

Timing and Festival Calendars

There was no universal festival calendar for all of ancient Greece. Each *polis* had its own customs and celebrations. However, of all the ancient calendars, we know most about the Athenian one.[2] The months were based on the phases of the moon, and there were normally twelve each year.[3] Aside from the annual and sometimes quadrennial festivals, certain days of each month were sacred to certain deities.[4] The sixth day of each month was sacred to Artemis,[5] and all of Her festivals except one[6] were held on the sixth of the month.

In order to create cohesive modern festivals, I drew from many but not all ancient ritual elements. Some seemed logistically impractical, while others were clearly parts of initiatory rites or rites of passage, and would be inefficiently used as part of a public celebration. Some of the ancient elements I used were Athenian, whereas others originated from other *poleis*. Because I began constructing festivals primarily using the Athenian calendar as a template, the Cataleos festivals appear to have an Athenian bias. However, I have over time included elements of festivals and customs from other *poleis*, and will most likely continue to do so. The Cataleos calendar itself could be considered a completely new set of festivals, as it is a fusion of many old and new elements. Even the ancient Athenian festivals I recreated without importing elements from other locations have still taken on a new meaning for the modern day.

Rather than catalogue each and every piece of evidence and explain why I did or did not choose to include it, I will instead only discuss those elements I did draw upon and leave the reader to explore the others on her own time. Much more could be said about each of the ancient festivals I will mention, but I must consider that beyond the scope of this book. For those interested in further reading, I shall include an ample annotated bibliography. I will limit my analysis of ancient ritual, and instead I will focus on our modern festivals, on what we can do now to celebrate Artemis, and how we can come to know Her better through those celebrations.

Many of the Cataleos festivals bear ancient names, and while they are generally similar to the ancient festivals and carry many of the same themes, the overall effect is probably quite different than what would have been experienced if we could travel back in time. This is, in my opinion, entirely appropriate. We are not ancient Greek people, and we do not live in ancient Greece. While the old myths and rituals can teach us a great deal about ourselves and about Artemis, we must still worship Her in a way that is appropriate for our own time, and that has the most significance to us.

Ritual Structure

There was no official ritual structure standard to all of ancient Greek religion, nor does one exist for the various modern permutations of Hellenismos. Each individual *polis* or city-state had its own particular customs and traditions, and each temple, shrine or sanctuary within each *polis* would have its own special rites and rituals. Similarly, today each modern group, temple, or organization tends to have its own rituals and customs. That said, most expressions of ancient Greek religion did share certain elements.

The typical ancient Greek festival consisted of a procession or *pompe*, a sacrifice, libations, and other offerings or activities particular to the deity and the festival. Musical performances and plays were also frequently included.[7] The ancient Greeks could turn almost anything into an *agon* or contest, and these games became a common and important feature of ancient festivals.[8] Purification played an important role in all types of ancient Greek rituals,[9] and almost all modern Hellenic ritual consists of some kind of purification, usually a *khernips* or hand-washing.

For modern festivals, I usually open with a ritual loosely based on *thusia*, an ancient Greek rite that I shall explore more thoroughly in chapter 4. I call this the Cataleos Opening Ritual, and it could be used to honor any Greek God, not just Artemis.

How To Do It: Cataleos Opening Ritual

For the basic opening ritual you will need a pitcher of water, a basket or container filled with barley, and an area to use as the ritual space. The ritual space itself can be as simple or as complicated as you like. A lovely spot in the woods can work just as well as an indoor temple space with an altar and a statue. A simple and easy ritual setup includes a small table to use as an altar, and some kind of fire on top of it. A candle or oil lamp works perfectly well, but I prefer to use a small or mid-sized cast iron tripod cauldron with a mixture of Epsom salt and isopropyl alcohol inside. This can create a small, relatively cool, clean-burning fire that is manageable indoors and outdoors. Always use caution when using fire in your rituals. Have safety equipment handy, and don't try something unless you're absolutely sure you can handle it safely.

You may also wish to have an image of Artemis in your ritual space. In ancient Greece, the statue would have been housed in the temple, whereas the altar and festival area were usually outside. You may wish to put an image on your altar anyway, or set up a separate table for the statue or image and other offerings. For rituals held outside the temple at Cataleos, I like to set up an altar in the center with the altar fire burning on top of it, and a shrine somewhere at the edge of the area with a statue, a libation bowl, a censer or incense holder and some incense, and space for people to leave other offerings.

It is also useful to have a hand towel waiting in the ritual space for use during the *khernips*, and an empty bowl as well is helpful for indoor rituals. The *khernips* is an act of purification for the participants, not for the ritual space. There is no purification performed on the space itself as part of the ritual, so if you feel that the space you're using ought to be cleansed prior to the ritual, you should do so before the festival begins. In ancient Greece festivals would be held in spaces that were already considered sacred or had already been purified and sanctified, so purification of the land itself as part of the festival was unnecessary. There were many ancient Greek methods of purifying an area, and there are many ways in which people accomplish this today, but such things are beyond the scope of this book.

As participants arrive at the festival location, you should first do any necessary preparation specific to the festival you will be celebrating. This is the time to create offerings and prepare other ritual items. Many people enjoy wearing special clothes for ritual; some will create ancient Greek clothes to wear, such as a *khiton* or *peplos*, whereas others have a favorite modern outfit or other special clothes they wear for festivals. Wreaths or garlands for the head called *stephanoi* are also popular, as they were almost universally worn during ancient Greek ritual. Today they can be made from natural flowers, artificial flowers, or twigs and branches from plants that have significance to the wearer.

You should also have someone designated as the acting priest or priestess. The issue of clergy is not one I shall address in depth in this book, as these days every group, temple, or organization has its own ways of determining who is a priest or priestess for their community, and what exactly that means and entails. For the purpose of these festivals, it is necessary only to designate someone as the acting priest or priestess for the length of the celebration. This person should be able to lead the group at critical moments, speak certain prayers on behalf of the congregation, and help the group transition from one activity to another while maintaining a continuous flow to the entire event. If the group already has a priest or priestess, particularly if he or she is a priest[10] or priestess of Artemis, then you would probably want to designate them as the acting priest or priestess for your festival. Alternatively, as the facilitator of the festival, you may want to take on this role yourself.

Once everything is ready, assemble everyone together for a procession. The procession itself should go from any convenient gathering place to the actual ritual space. It can be as short as walking from the kitchen to the living room, or as long as a trek through the woods. First in line goes someone carrying the barley, and second goes someone carrying the water. There is no official order for people after these two, but whoever is acting as priest or priestess usually goes third (if he or she is not already carrying barley or water), and others follow after in what order they will. I frequently include some of the festival-specific offerings as part of the opening ritual, and I instruct people to carry those with them in the procession. The barley and water bearers may choose either to carry both the barley or water and their offerings, or have someone carry their offerings in for them.

When the procession arrives at the ritual space, everyone should end up standing in a circle around the altar. One way to accomplish this is to have the whole procession circle the altar once. You may wish to let people set down their offerings (I will discuss convenient locations as we cover each of the individual festival offerings), as they will need their hands during the opening ritual. If people want to hold on to their offerings until it is time to offer them, they can always tuck them into a pocket or a convenient fold of their clothing.

When performing rituals and festivals in a space that is not usually set aside for sacred use, I like to begin with an apotropaic exclamation: "Hekas! Hekas! Apotrepete kakon! Far away! Far away! Turn away evil!"[11] This cry is meant to drive away any lingering energies or entities that do not belong in a ritual honoring the Gods. A space that is always reserved for religious activity, such as a temple or a special room set aside for worship, would already keep out such entities and energies and the cry would not be necessary.

Next, the two individuals carrying the barley and the water process around the entire ritual space and all the offerings and participants within it. This can be performed by anyone you choose, but there are some important factors to consider when you make your choice. The point of processing the barley and water around the congregation and ritual area is not to sanctify the space, but to define it and to declare that sacred acts shall occur within it. When doing this myself, I usually say a few words aloud explaining the action: "With barley and water we define this holy space. The sacred is delineated from the profane, and we declare that all acts performed within shall be sacred and pleasing to the Gods." This proclamation goes beyond a simple explanation and becomes a statement of intent. We are only human, and mortals are fallible. We can't expect to do everything right every single time, but we always try our best. With this statement we tell the Gods that our intent is to honor Them with all that we do, and we hope that even if something doesn't go exactly right, They will still be pleased by our effort. Thus, when choosing who shall carry the barley and water around the circle, be sure to select someone who can thoroughly express this sentiment not only for themselves, but also on behalf of everyone present.

Furthermore, you may wish to consider the particular meaning and attributes of the barley and water as ritual tools when you choose their carriers. The container of barley is a tool of sacrifice. In a *thusia* ritual it would have concealed the sacrificial knife, and the grains of barley would have been thrown at the sacrifice itself. Even when the barley is not being used in this way, it still reminds us of these practices, and thus also reminds us that all things worth having come at a price, a necessary sacrifice. The water is a simple and universal tool of purification. It washes away dirt and carries away our impurities to leave us cleansed, refreshed, renewed, and fit to be in the presence of the Gods. It is a symbol of all things pure and holy, and of the power of purification. You may wish to consider all of these things when choosing barley-bearers and water-bearers, or you may choose to have two people process with the barley and water, and two different people circumambulate with them. You may even choose to be one of those people yourself. Consider the particular needs and resources of your own group and decide what will work best for you.

After marking out the sacred space, it's time for *khernips,* or hand-washing. Have either the water-bearer or the acting priest or priestess pour water over the hands of each of the participants. You may choose to say some words about the purifying powers of water and washing, or just let the action speak for itself. Once everyone else has washed, have someone switch with the person pouring the water so that they too can wash. For outdoor rituals, it works perfectly well to have each of the participants hold out their hands and pour the water over them and onto the ground. For indoor rituals, you can have another person carry around the empty bowl, holding it under each person's hands as the water is poured over them. Once everyone's hands have been washed, be sure the bowl of used water gets placed outside the ritual space, as it now contains all the impurities the participants cast off. The water bearer should also carry around the hand towel, perhaps folded over one arm, so that participants have a clean way to dry their hands after washing. (Some people prefer to simply have a bowl of water that each person dips their hands into to wash for *khernips*. I dislike this idea because after the first person washes, everyone else will be putting their hands into sullied water.)

After *khernips,* the acting priest or priestess should light the altar fire. I usually do this in solemn silence with mindfulness and due respect for both the element of fire and for the significance of the holy flame upon Artemis' altar.

Next is what I have come to call the barley prayer. Have the barley bearer or the acting priest or priestess carry the basket of barley around to each of the participants, and have each person take some barley and hold it in their hand. Once everyone has a handful of barley, the acting priest or priestess should speak a prayer relevant to the event. If you are gathered for a festival of Artemis, say something about why that festival is important to you and your group, why you bother celebrating it, what you hope to gain from it, and offer your worship as a gift to Artemis. When the prayer is complete, everyone all at once should throw their barley at the altar fire. You will probably want to explain this to people as you hand out the barley, and instruct participants to focus on the prayer as they hold their handful of barley and silently add their own intent. By having everyone throw their barley at the fire together, the prayer of one person is transformed into a communal act in which everyone participates. If you are using a candle as your altar fire, you may wish to have people throw their barley at the altar rather than at the flame itself. This is admittedly one of the reasons I prefer to have a cauldron with filled with fire on the altar rather than a candle; it allows people to actually throw their barley into the fire.

The barley prayer marks the culmination of the Cataleos Opening Ritual. I usually continue with one of the festival-specific offerings made while everyone is gathered together in the ritual space, and then move on to other festival activities.

Theoxenia

I usually end festivals with a ritual I like to call *Theoxenia*. It is basically a pot-luck feast, which ancient festivals would have culminated in,[12] only I also set out a plate for Artemis (and, in the case of joint festivals, for the other deities honored as well). I offer Her a small portion, hopefully the best, from each dish, allowing other people present to contribute to it as well if they like. This is not an entirely original concept; in certain cases Zeus Philios or the Dioskouroi were honored at feasts in which a place was prepared and food offered for Them. It is from these rituals that I borrow the term *Theoxenia* and the concept for the rite.[13] I also include in this a final libation reminiscent of the Homeric formula for ending a festival.[14]

How To Do It: Cataleos Theoxenia

A Theoxenia ritual is a simple, easy, and effective way to end a festival. You will need a special plate and cup or libation bowl for Artemis, and a pot luck feast to share with everyone. Have everyone gather together and set out the food they brought for the feast. When everyone is assembled and all the food is ready, take the special plate and put on it one small portion from every dish, hopefully the best part of each. When the plate is full, have the acting priest or priestess say a prayer to Artemis. The prayer should be something relevant not only the festival you just celebrated, but also to your particular celebration of it. If something especially potent or enjoyable happened, mention that and thank Her for it. Invite Artemis to join the feast, and thank Her for sharing Her feast with you. When the prayer is complete, the acting priest or priestess should pour a libation of the best drink available into the special cup, then place the plate and cup somewhere special for Artemis – perhaps in the center of the table, or before a special chair or place that has been set for Her, or at a shrine made for Her. Invite people to add food offerings to the plate or give their own libations as they wish.

There does not need to be any official end or closing of the feast. Allow people to relax and enjoy the food and each other's company. Festivals are meant to built community as well as honor the Gods. Encourage festival-relevant discussion, but don't force it. If your time at the festival location is limited, politely let people know when it's time to clean up and go home. Otherwise, allow people to enjoy the event until each person decides to take their leave.

The Six Festivals of Artemis Cataleos

1: Arkteia

Life-sized statue of a little girl dedicated to Artemis Brauronia. (Archaeological Museum of Vravrona)

The Ancient Festival

The cult of Artemis Brauronia remains largely mysterious to us today. We have very little literary evidence to work with, and the archaeological evidence is tantalizing but inconclusive. The cult originated at Brauron[15], located on the eastern coast of Attica. In the sixth century B.C.E. Peisistratos founded the Brauronion on the Athenian acropolis, a sanctuary dependent on the cult center in Brauron.[16]

The ancient Brauronia festival was celebrated in Athens every four years[17]. It included a procession of women to Brauron[18], and a rite called the *arkteia* in which little girls acted like bears.[19] Some kind of *arkteia* was probably celebrated all over Attica,[20] and these smaller rites probably had a more personal significance than the community-oriented *arkteia* of the Athenian festival.[21] The foundation myth for the cult of Artemis Braruonia gives a possible explanation for this rite:

> ...a she-bear frequented the neighborhood and was tamed and lived in the sanctuary. A young girl who was playing with it teased it so that in its rage it tore out one of her eyes. Her brothers in revenge killed it. But the goddess's anger had been roused and a plague followed. When the oracle was consulted for a remedy, the Athenians were told to make their daughters act the she-bear as an atonement. So the Athenians voted that a maiden might not be wedded before she had performed this ritual.[22]

At Brauron at least we know that the *arkteia* began with girls wearing saffron-colored robes that were shed over the course of the rite,[23] although Vernant guesses that younger girls went nude while older girls were clothed.[24] The purpose of the *arkteia* was supposedly to prepare girls for marriage. A young girl, believed by the ancient Greeks to be wild by nature, would act the bear in honor of Artemis, and by channeling that wildness into acceptable ritual, eventually be tamed and made ready for marriage.[25] The rite may also have been considered to appease Artemis, diverting the anger She would otherwise show towards girls who gave up their virginity.[26]

What is certain is that bears played an important role in the cult of Artemis Brauronia,[27] and so would have been involved in Her festivals as well. The myth of Artemis and Callisto may have been involved, perhaps in the form of a dramatization.[28] Little girls probably ran or danced in honor of Artemis, sometimes carrying twigs,[29] and this may have been synonymous with the *arkteia.*[30] Small goblets called *krateriskoi* were probably used to hold water which was sprinkled using twigs or small branches.[31] There are many theories regarding the meaning of each of these activities, but no one truly knows with certainty.

There is ample evidence for other various ritual activities, but we cannot yet put them together into a cohesive picture of any festival or festivals. Many of the activities represented on ancient pottery or alluded to in ancient literary sources may have been rites of passage rather than activities for public festival.

When creating a modern Arkteia festival I chose not only to include elements from what we know of the ancient festival, but also elements from the cult of Artemis Brauronia in general. It was to Brauron that Athenian girls were sent to serve Artemis,[32] and during my own visit to the site and museum at Brauron, now called Vravrona, I saw for myself the many statuettes of girls and boys found at the sanctuary. Here, as elsewhere, Artemis acted as a protectress of all children rather than of girls only,[33] and also as a goddess of childbirth.[34]

During my visit to Brauron I was surprised by the number of depictions of Artemis that showed Her with a torch rather than a bow. In particular I remember a beautiful statuette of Artemis Hekate[35]. It shows three female figures standing back to back, one with a torch in her right hand and raising her *khiton* with her left, one with a torch in her left hand and her right hand held to her breast, and the third with a torch in each hand. This was found in the retaining wall of the Sanctuary of Artemis Brauronia,[36] and along with the various other reliefs it show that Artemis's light-bringer aspect had some importance at Brauron.

There is one last element of ancient worship that I should mention, since even though it was not a specifically Artemisian practice, I chose to use it for the modern Arkteia festival. In ancient Greece it was quite common for worshippers to hang woolen strips or ribbons on statues of the Gods as an act of adoration and prayer.[37] This form of worship was not specific to any particular God or festival, and could be used for almost any deity at any time.

The sanctuary of Artemis Brauronia.

The Modern Arkteia

The very first time I tried to run a festival based on the cult of Artemis Brauronia, I tried to keep the original intent of the festival as a rite of passage. Adults were invited to embrace their inner child through ritual, and then by dedicating childish toys to Artemis, pass again into adulthood with Her blessing. I called the festival Brauronia, and it was a flop. I ran the festival at a private Pagan gathering, and although many people expressed interest beforehand, only one person actually showed up specifically because she wanted to honor Artemis. Other people came, but more to support me than to honor Her. However, despite the fact that the festival did not appeal to the general populace, it was still a thoroughly enjoyable celebration. I did my best to create something that would please the people present, and a little girl and her caretaker just happened to show up and join us, helping everyone get into the childish spirit.

At the end of the day as I was packing up all the ritual tools and carrying them back to my car, I saw a doe and her fawn watching me in the woods. I was able to get remarkably close to them, just to watch and admire their beauty. As far as I was concerned, it had to be a sign. The fact that we had just celebrated Artemis as the protectress of children, and now I was seeing not only one of Her sacred animals but its young as well, seemed all too appropriate to me. I knew Artemis was pleased with my efforts, and I knew that the general idea of a Brauronian festival was a good one, even if I hadn't gotten it quite right.

Over the next year I intensified my research on the cult of Artemis at Brauron and reinvented the modern festival. People seemed to really enjoy playing childish games at my first attempt, and in a society where so much pressure is put on us to behave properly and act like adults, I thought it would be a very good idea to have a festival aimed at helping people cut loose and embrace their inner child. I renamed the new modern festival Arkteia, and it was immediately popular.

We each have within us a child that can be a source of creativity and jubilant energy. The pressures of everyday life and adult concerns repress that youthful joy, sometimes so thoroughly that we forget it's even there. Celebrating the Arkteia gives us a socially acceptable way to act like children and enjoy it. We can play the games we are too embarrassed to admit we still like. We can paint and draw and color and not care about staying in the lines or making our picture look like anything at all if that pleases us. We can run and jump and play and do what we like simply because we like doing it. We don't need adult reasons for why we are rolling around in the grass or climbing a tree or making a sand castle. It's just a fun thing to do, and that's enough.

The ancient Greek perception that girls needed to go through a ritual like the *arkteia* in order to be readied for marriage comes in part from their perspective on the nature of women in general. In a previously published essay entitled *The Virgin Goddess*,[38] I explained how the ancient Greeks believed the human body to be symmetrical not only horizontally but vertically as well. Thus, a man was a purely projective being, pouring forth his essence from both his genitalia and his mouth, whereas a woman was a purely receptive being, receiving the essence of men. When a woman had sex with a man, she would be forever after contaminated by his essence; nothing she did or said from then on was truly her own – or so the ancient Greeks believed.

In light of this we can see that Artemis's virginity has more to do with independence and freedom than it does with sex itself. As Burkert explains, "...the virginity of Artemis is not asexuality as is Athena's practical and organizational intelligence, but a peculiarly erotic and challenging ideal."[39] Our cultural understanding of sex and its role in modern society have changed dramatically from that of the ancient Greeks. Thus, a modern woman might decide that it is perfectly Artemisian of her to sleep with whomever she chooses. Because sex, relationships, and marriage can now have such vastly different meanings for each person, this is an issue best left for each individual to work out between themselves and Artemis.

Even so, in mythology Artemis remains untouched by any kind of sexual activity.[40] Her abstinence becomes a symbol of the purity of nature:

> A feeling for virgin nature with meadows, groves, and mountains, which are as yet barely articulated elsewhere, begins to find form here; Artemis is the goddess of the open countryside beyond the towns and villages and beyond the fields tilled in the works of men.[41]

Artemis the wild, untamed virgin is a direct manifestation of the wilderness of nature into which no human has set foot.

The ancient Greeks believed that young girls were just as wild as Artemis was. In order to be married off to a civilized Greek man (as they believed all women should be[42]), young women had to be tamed, just as an expanse of land had to be cleared and plowed before it could be farmed. This understanding was intrinsic to their time and culture, and does not necessarily apply to the modern day.

I do not believe that women need to be tamed to exist happily in modern society. As far as I'm concerned, that aspect of the ancient *Arkteia* is one that no longer applies to modern culture. However, I do believe there is still good reason for dancing the bear dance and celebrating the modern Arkteia with that traditional rite. The vast majority of modern day citizens in the United States of America live a life that is far removed from the natural world. We reside in cities and suburbs, buy our food at grocery markets, and go to schools and desk jobs. We rarely see the primordial world of nature that still supports us beneath all the trappings of technology and civilization. When I dance the Arkteia, it is to embrace and express the wildness within myself. It reminds me that I am an animal, just like every other creature on this Earth. I may be smart enough to drive a car and use a computer, but deep down inside I am a wild creature of nature, and to forget that is to disrespect the natural world that created and sustains me. At the Arkteia I celebrate the natural wilderness around me as well as my own wild nature.

I know of no official date when the ancient *Arkteia* festival was celebrated. When I held that first Brauronia ritual, it was in early October because that happened to be the time of the private pagan gathering where I thought I would have the resources to put it on. However, as I revised the festival and as the Cataleos calendar developed, it became clear that spring was a much better time for a modern Arkteia. I felt that spring would be a good time to celebrate youthfulness and renewal, and March would be a good month in which to embrace and express wild energies. Thus the official date of the modern Arkteia festival became March sixth.

Celebrating the Arkteia

To create a Cataleos-style Arkteia festival, you will need enough yellow ribbon such that each participant can have a piece, a small leafy branch from a birch tree, an additional bowl of pure water, one small model bear for each participant or enough clay or other crafting material such that each participant can make their own model bear, some childish games to play, and one tea light or votive candle for each participant. You will also need to have some kind of image or statue of Artemis in your ritual space, and some method by which participants can attach their ribbons to it. A simple way to achieve this is to tie a cord around the waist of your statue or statuette, or around the center of your image, as if it were a belt or a girdle. Participants can then slip their ribbon through the cord to attach it to the image. Alternatively, you may wish to go with the traditional method of using a bit of wax to stick the ribbon to the statue.

You will also need to locate a place outdoors where your group can go to embrace the wild. Every city has a park in it somewhere, and most have nature reserves hidden away in unlikely places. Do a search online, or ask people who know your area well, and find someplace you can go outdoors that gets you as close to nature as possible.

As participants arrive, have them select or create their model bear and cut their piece of ribbon. Explain that the bears will be given as an offering to Artemis the Goddess of Wilderness and Wild Things along with any prayer they wish to say to Her. Encourage them to personalize their bears and put the intent of their prayers into them. If you are using pre-made bears rather than making them yourselves, consider having markers or paints available so that people can decorate and personalize their offering. Explain to participants that the ribbon will be used as an offering given to Artemis while each participant asks for the protection of a child, children, or pregnant woman they care about. The size of each piece of ribbon does not need to be specific. Let each person choose their own length, but suggest that it be long enough to effectively attach to the statue and short enough that everyone can have some.

Once the bears and ribbons are ready, have everyone gather for the procession and begin with the Cataleos Opening Ritual. Participants will not need their bears until later, but have them carry their ribbons with them in the opening procession. You should have the birch branch and the extra bowl of water waiting in the ritual space.

When the barley prayer is done, have the acting priest or priestess say a few words appealing to Artemis the Protectress of Children and Helper in Childbirth. Have each participant think of the children or women they want to pray for. Then, one by one, have each person go up to the image or statue and attach their ribbon to it, either saying their prayer out loud or thinking it silently. When everyone has placed their ribbon, have the acting priest or priestess once again speak on behalf of the group, reiterating the general sentiment of the prayers. Ask Artemis to protect the children and pregnant women you care about, to keep them safe and healthy. Explain that you have given Her ribbons as gifts in return for Her protection, and express your hope that She will find them pleasing.

Next have the acting priest or priestess speak of spring. It is a time of refreshing renewal, of youth and exuberance and unrestrained growth and joy, but in order to make room for new growth, we much cast away that which clutters our lives and holds us back. Have each person think of something that hinders them, something they don't need and want help getting rid of. Then have the acting priest or priestess go to each person with the birch branch and the bowl of water. Tell each participant to ask Artemis to help them get rid of what they want to loose as the acting priest or priestess dips the birch branch in the water and sprinkles the participant with it, asking Artemis to wash away that which hinders us. You could also opt to have each participant take the birch branch and sprinkle themselves with water as they ask Artemis for Her help. Some groups enjoy having the help and guidance of a leading figure, whereas others prefer celebrations that are as equally participatory as possible. You must determine which is best for your group.

Once everyone has been thoroughly cleansed and refreshed, having cast away the clutter of another year, it's time to get outside and embrace the wild. Take your group to some place that is close to nature. Find a trail and go for a hike, or enjoy a secluded spot where you can actually observe your local wildlife. Near the temple of Artemis at Cataleos is the Middlesex Fells Reservation, a patch of wooded wilderness just a short drive from the city. I discovered that within the Fells is a little place called Bear Hill, and I felt that was all too appropriate for a festival celebrating Artemis Brauronia. Consequently, when we go out to embrace nature at the Cataleos Arkteia, we take a hike up to the top of Bear Hill.

Any type of nature can be an appropriate place to embrace the wild. If you live near the desert, find an area where all you can see are rocks and sand and cacti. If you live on the coast, perhaps an unpopulated, undeveloped beach will reveal the natural world to you. Any area that shows as little human influence as possible is a good place to go. When we reach the top of Bear Hill, I give us all some time to wander about and enjoy being outdoors. Once everyone has had a chance to enjoy the natural world a bit, I call the group back together and speak a prayer to Artemis the Goddess of Wilderness and Wild Things. I invite each person to say their own prayer to Her, aloud or silently, and offer their little bear.

When you do this yourself, you can choose any spot you like for the bear offerings. Explore your chosen place of wilderness before the ritual and look for a spot that calls to you, that feels particularly sacred or infused with Artemisian energy. If you are unsure, ask Her for a sign. Sometimes an animal will pop out of the woods at a certain place to show you where She wants you to go. You may decide that everyone should leave their bears on top of a special rock or at the foot of a special tree, or you may choose to let each person decide where to leave their bear.

Now that you are outside enjoying nature, it's time to share your favorite version of the myth of Artemis and Callisto. Perhaps you will have someone tell the myth as you all travel back to where you will celebrate the rest of your festival, or perhaps you would enjoy putting on a full dramatization. Choose whichever method appeals most to you and your group.

There are many, many versions of the myth of Artemis and Callisto. All of these start with Callisto, sometimes a mortal woman and sometimes a nymph, being a companion of Artemis who captures the attention of Zeus. Zeus manages to have sex with Callisto; according to some He does this against her will in His own form, whereas according to others He does so disguised as Apollo or even Artemis. Callisto becomes pregnant and tries to conceal this from Artemis, but eventually Artemis discovers the deception when Callisto is bathing. According to some versions, Artemis shot her for this, but most versions say that Artemis turned Callisto into a bear. Some versions say that Hera then persuaded Artemis to shoot the bear not knowing it was really Callisto. When Artemis discovered who She had just killed, She convinced Zeus to place her in the sky as a constellation. In other versions it was Hera who turned Callisto into a bear when she willingly has sex with Zeus, and then Hera convinced Artemis to unknowingly kill Callisto.[43]

It's important to pause a moment here and consider why we bother with ancient myths at all. Many people feel that it's better to use modern retellings of the ancient myths, as they are more fitting to our own day and time. I believe that this idea is not in and of itself a bad one, but I am frequently disappointed and dissatisfied with modern versions of the ancient myths. There's a reason the ancient myths have survived for thousands of years: there is some truth hidden within them that transcends time and culture. As much as we may feel that our own modern versions are just as valuable and hold just as much truth, I will remain skeptical until they too have persisted for thousands of years.

Almost every ancient Greek myth comes in various different versions, and frequently they seem to contradict one another. In fact, just about everything in ancient Greek religion seems self-contradictory or even paradoxical on some level. However, I have found beneath the surface of any myth there is always a theme that is true for all versions, some underlying truth that is expressed by each permutation of the tale. Even seemingly contradictory or paradoxical ancient Greek beliefs and practices ultimately express a greater truth; two opposing aspects of a deity are perhaps really just opposite sides of the same coin, and a seemingly self-contradictory ritual practice actually expresses a deep truth about the differences between mortality and divinity. A piece of ancient evidence is almost never as simple as it seems on the surface, and someone who immediately discards an ancient myth or source simply because they don't understand or relate to it right away will end up missing a lot.

All that said, I do believe that modern renditions of ancient myths can be useful, valuable, and insightful. I simply feel that they must express the same underlying message as all the other versions. It's certainly true that we live in a very different time and culture than that of the ancient Greeks, and the ancient myths were created within the cultural context of their own time. If we attempt to interpret the myths at face value, it will be difficult (if not impossible) to discover their true meaning, as the actions of mythological figures mean very different things to us today than they would have meant to the ancient Greeks. I prefer to study ancient Greek culture until I understand the context of a myth well enough to catch a glimpse of what it might have meant to the ancient Greek people. This often allows me to see how seemingly contradictory versions are actually not contradictory at all, or how what appears to be the message of a particular myth is actually entirely beside the point. This approach, however, is not for everyone, and it is not the only way to discover the underlying meaning of a myth. Thus I can see great value in retelling the same story within a modern context as long as the original message is carried through.

The trouble with this is not just ascertaining what the original message of a myth was to begin with, but also finding a way to accurately express it. The myths are stories that carry sacred truths about ourselves and about the Gods. They are not necessarily literally true in and of themselves, but they point to truth. Finding a way to express a truth you have discovered to someone else is extremely difficult. Even when ten different people all understand the same exact concept, they will all express it in a different way. We may each feel that we have come to understand the underlying message of a myth, and we may each be correct, but we will probably also attempt to express that message in vastly different ways, and our ways may not be useful to anyone outside our own community, or our own group, or our own circle of friends, or even to anyone besides ourselves. This is, in my mind, what is so remarkable about the ancient Greek myths. They have found a way to express various truths to millions of people in hundreds of different cultures over thousands of years. Again, when a modern myth has withstood a similar test, I will hold it in as high regard.

After sharing your group's favorite rendition of the myth of Callisto, it's time to unleash your wild side and dance the bear. For some this can be the most challenging festival activity. Some people find it wonderfully easy to just get up and dance, whereas others are self-conscious about their body and its movements, and find it difficult to express themselves freely through motion.

The bear dance is meant to be an unbridled expression of your own inner wild nature. We live in a modern society where we must act within some range of socially accepted norms in order to live a productive life; there can be many deviations within that range, but to some extent we all must bend to the rules of society. For example, the inner wildness of one person may tell him or her that it is right and good to go walking down the street completely naked, but if he or she does not bend to the social norm of wearing clothes, they are likely to make a visit to the local police station. By dancing our wildness in the Arkteia, we find an acceptable way to express our yearning for complete freedom while still living within the laws and cultural customs of our civilization.

Any type of dance can be appropriate for the Arkteia. People can leap and jump, writhe around, make shuffling bear-like steps, or perform some other dance they feel most comfortable with. Anything that allows unrestrained, expressive motion is perfectly appropriate. Similarly, any type of music can be used to accompany it. A simple drumbeat may be all you need, or your group may choose to sing along with your dance. Music can be a wonderful source of motivation for a group that finds it difficult to get up and dance. Find a piece of music that appeals to you and the people you will be celebrating with, be it reconstructed ancient music, modern pop or rock, or anything else you can think of. When it comes time to dance the bear, play your song. If you can, play it loudly! Hearing the thumping vibrations of the song in your body might help inspire you and your group to get up and dance.

Alternatively, some groups might be better inspired by a guided meditation. I think a combination of music and meditation can be powerfully motivating. If your group has a hard time getting into the dance, try this: Take your group to an open, private space, where you can all get up and move freely but not have to worry about being seen by outsiders. This could be a secluded spot outdoors, or a spacious private room. Select a piece of music that is suited to your group, and have it ready to play. Tell each participant to sit or lie down comfortably. Take a few breaths together to relax, then read them the following guided meditation:

> Imagine yourself in a deep forest. Smell the scent of evergreen mixed with rich earth. Feel warm speckles of sunshine falling through the shady trees. Enjoy your wooded retreat. Feel free from any constraints or expectations.
>
> Suddenly you see a figure darting between the trees. At first you catch only a glimpse of Her as She darts in and out of the foliage, but She is drawing closer to you, and you can hear the pulse of Her dance.
>
> *[begin playing the music now, softly at first, growing slowly louder]*
>
> Watch Her dance around you, weaving Her way through the forest. Feel the dance call to you. Feel the urge to join and follow Her, and when you are ready, rise and dance with us.

Allow people as much time as they need to join in the dancing. Some people may not feel comfortable enough to get up and physically dance, but will instead perform their own inner dance. Do what you can to get to know your group beforehand, and be prepared for unusual results. Some groups find guided meditations such as this extremely helpful, while others do not. Again, you must consider the particular needs of your own group and figure out how to best present each activity to the particular people present at your festival.

Next comes what most people consider to be the best part of an Arkteia festival: childish games! Play together! Play anything you want. If you like board games, bring some of your favorite board games from when you were a child and share them with the group. Invite participants beforehand to bring along any childhood games they enjoy. Go outside with a piece of chalk and a stone and play hopscotch. If there's a playground nearby, take your group there to swing, slide and climb. If you're near an open field, play tag or bring along a ball to play whatever games or sports you like. If the weather is poor, get a big coloring book or some blank paper, and have fun with paints, crayons and markers. Arts and crafts kits designed specifically for children are inexpensive, easy to get, and great fun. You could even give participants the option to dedicate their creations to Artemis. Anything at all that encourages a childish, playful spirit is entirely appropriate.

While I do like to have this time in the festival set aside specifically for games and childish activities, do not feel that you need to confine such things to this section of the festival. Whenever there is down time between parts of the ritual, encourage people to play. If some people take longer than others making their bears and cutting their ribbon, start a game with the others. If you have a long drive to your wilderness spot, play a game of "I Spy" in the car. The options are limitless and flexible; be as creative with them as you can be.

Once everyone has had their fill of running around like children, gather your group for a Theoxenia and enjoy a meal together. Once everyone has finished eating, invite each of the participants to take a tea light or votive candle. Say a final prayer to Artemis Phosphoros, the light bringer, and to Artemis Hekate, She Who can guide us through uncertain times and difficult terrain, Who can show us how to embrace wildness without falling into madness. Instruct participants to go into the ritual space alone, one at a time. Tell them to speak their own private prayer to Artemis, light their candle, and leave it there as an offering for Her.

When people can't physically make it to the Arkteia festival but still want to celebrate with the Cataleos community, I host a charity project through the website, usually benefiting one of the local battered women's shelters or wildlife rehabilitation organizations. If you are unable to summon a group together to celebrate the Arkteia, consider contributing to the Cataleos charity project, or perhaps hold one of your own charity events applicable to a group in your area. Find out about your local charity groups and choose one whose mission and methods you feel fit with Artemisian ideals and the overall concept of the Arkteia. Ask what that charity needs, and do what you can to help out.

The goal of the Arkteia is to help people understand the aspects of Artemis that protect, nurture, and liberate. With Her help at the Arkteia, participants can hopefully learn a bit more about their own wild nature, embrace their inner child and keep it a little closer to the surface, and release some pent up tension through expressive motion. At the end of the day, participants should go home feeling freer, wilder, and filled with childish joy.

2: Mounukhia

Artemis Hekate. (Archaeological Museum of Vravrona)

The Ancient Festival

The ancient Athenians celebrated a festival in honor of Artemis Mounukhia on the 16th of their month of *Mounukhion.*[44] The epithet Mounukhia comes from a steep hill just inland over Peiraeus, over which Artemis presides,[45] and the name of the hill supposedly came from the name of the hero, Mounikhios, who founded the cult of Artemis there.[46] In fact, the foundation myth of this cult was probably connected to one of the ancient festival activities: a goat sacrifice.[47]

> The story ran that a she-bear had entered the shrine where it was killed by the Athenians. This act roused the wrath of the goddess, who brought a plague on them as a punishment. The oracle was consulted and declared that the remedy would be found if someone sacrificed his daughter to Artemis. This response naturally created a reluctance to comply, until a man named Embaros volunteered to satisfy the oracle, if he and his family were awarded the priesthood of the goddess for life. He solved the problem of the sacrifice by a naively simple trick. He

> brought his daughter to the shrine as though to offer her and hid her in the innermost sanctuary. He then produced a she-goat dressed up like his daughter and sacrificed it.[48]

It is certainly significant that Artemis ultimately accepts the goat and the plague is ended. From then on, the Athenians are told to sacrifice as Embaros did, thus with a goat instead of a girl.[49]

The most well known element of the ancient Mounukhia festival is the procession and dedication of *amphiphontes*, special cakes decorated with little torches.[50] These cakes are mentioned in a fragment from a comedy by Philemon called *The Poor Girl* or *The Girl from Rhodes*: "Artemis, dear mistress, to you I carry, lady, this cake shining all around and what is to serve as a drink-offering."[51] Parke remarks that ancient commentators saw these cakes as being symbolic of the moon,[52] and the timing of this festival suggests lunar connections as well, as the sixteenth would have been close to or at the time the full moon.[53] In fact, the Mounukhia is the only Athenian festival of Artemis we know of held on any day other than the sixth, which strengthens the argument that there is some importance to it being held on the sixteenth instead. Clearly this festival celebrated Artemis as a light-bringer, and probably as a lunar Goddess as well.

Mock naval battles were also featured in the ancient Mounukhia celebration, and this too is connected to celebrating Artemis as a lunar Goddess. As Vernant explains:

> "The 16th day of Mounikhion," Plutarch says, "the Athenians consider sacred to Artemis, because on that day the goddess shone as a full moon for the Greeks who were victorious at Salamis [*epelampsen he theos panselenos*]," (*Mor*. 349f).[54]

However, Simon notes that the battle of Salamis was actually fought seven months earlier, but it was celebrated as part of the Mounukhia festival because Artemis Mounukhia helped the Athenians against the Persian fleet. This was commemorated with mock sea battles called *naumakhia*.[55]

It may at first seem odd that Artemis was called upon for victory in a naval battle, or that She was honored with boat fights and worshipped at a harbor. However, in Callimachus we learn that Artemis was "watcher over streets and harbors,"[56] so it is actually not strange at all that She would be honored at Mounukhia and Peiraeus, or celebrated with sea battles.

There were a few other ancient celebrations I drew from to create a modern Mounukhia festival. On the 6th day of *Mounukhion*, a procession of girls walked to the Delphinion, a shrine near the Ilissos where both Artemis and Apollo were worshipped. Each girl carried an olive branch bound with white wool. Simon calls this festival *Hiketeria* ("suppliant's twig") after the bound branches, and both Simon and Parke suppose that these were meant for Artemis, and perhaps the whole festival was held in Her honor.[57] Park even suggests that this was probably meant to appeal to Artemis for the protection of girls and women.[58]

Everywhere in ancient Greece, dancing was a part of women's lives and ritual activities. This is particularly true of Artemisian ritual.

> Everywhere girls approaching marriageable age come together to form dancing groups, especially at festivals in honour of the goddess [Artemis]; this is in fact one of the most important opportunities for young men to become acquainted with girls.[59]

It is possible that some dancing groups, particularly those that gathered at the borders of an area, would hang terracotta figurines of girls from a tree. These would have been apotropaic figures meant to gain Artemis' protection.[60]

In the Athenian month of *Thargelion*, a festival called the *Bendidia* was held in honor of the Thracian Goddess Bendis, Whom the Athenians equated with Artemis. This was an all-night celebration of which relay races were a part.[61] While foot races in which a torch was passed along the participants were common in Attica, the race at the *Bendidia* was done on horseback. Parke guesses that this was an innovation of the Thracians.[62]

From right to left: Apollo, Leto, Artemis holding a torch, an altar, and a group of worshipers. (Archaeological Museum of Vravrona)

The Modern Mounukhia

The modern Mounukhia festival has taken on a decidedly feminist theme. This is true not only of the Cataleos Mounukhia celebration; I discovered recently that other Hellenic groups celebrating their own permutation of the Mounukhia have also spontaneously decided to add feminist themes to their festivals. There is certainly plenty of evidence for feminist worship in Artemisian cult, but as far as I can tell, this was not a part of the original Athenian Mounukhia festival. Nevertheless it has evolved independently in multiple areas as part of our modern Mounukhia, and I am thoroughly convinced that it is a needed and positive addition that Artemis is pleased with.

It seems to me that there are many modern non-reconstructionist Neo-Pagan groups that wish to honor Artemis as a Goddess of feminism, but do so in a way that rejects all men. They seem to view

Artemis as a Goddess who disdains or even despises men. I will certainly not judge the validity or value of this point of view, but I will point out that it is absolutely not based on ancient evidence. Men and women both worshipped Artemis in ancient Greece,[63] and She showed favor to both genders.[64] In mythology, Her "best friend" among all mortals was a man named Hippolytos.[65] Thus, I believe that these modern groups may indeed worship a very real and powerful Goddess who scorns men, but She is not, in my opinion, the same Artemis of the ancient Greeks.

The above statement obviously raises controversy. People immediately ask "what right does any human have to say what the Gods are or are not?" Oinokhoe has already answered this question more eloquently than I could have myself:

> Well, obviously, no one can say *for sure*. However, we can say with some modicum of reasonability. You have to draw a line somewhere. If we accept every person's version of a god/dess, no matter how far it veers from the collective understanding of thousands of people over thousands of years, then we might as well just not speak of specific gods at all by name, and just talk about "a goddess of ___" and let everyone interpret it to their heart's desire. Again, we have to draw a line...
>
> If you just accept everyone's experiences as equally valid when it comes to the actual gods themselves, then I guess you won't correct someone who says that Demeter is actually a male god, or that Poseidon rules over forests instead of oceans, or that Dionysos requires sobriety from his worshipers. I mean, if you're going to accept some total rejections of tradition, you'll have to accept them all. Sure, there's room for some variation and UPG [unsubstantiated personal gnosis], but at some point one has to say, "That's no longer recognizably the god that everyone else is talking about."[66]

As I wrote earlier, I do not claim to have the One Truth about Who or What Artemis is, nor do I believe there is only one valid point of view. That said, I do have my opinions about Who She is and is not. I am entitled to my opinions, and I offer to share them with willing readers. If you don't like my ideas, don't read my book.

The feminism of a Cataleos Mounukhia ritual is one where men are invited and welcome to participate, but only if they wish to show their support for women and for feminism. The Mounukhia celebrates feminine power as a force that is equal to masculine power, but that is also a different, wild strength that is entirely independent of men and masculinity. There are moments in the festival when men stand by silently and allow women to act alone, and there are moments when men play a supporting role that enhances the women's experience. The point is to recognize women as strong, independent agents that can act with or without the support of men, but also to appreciate and include those men who choose to support and empower women. Men can be feminists too; they can fight for women's rights, find various ways to support the women around them, or even simply stand down at times and give women the space to act alone. Men's cooperation and support can enhance women's fight for equality and independence. We do not need to entirely rebuff men in order to secure feminine strength.

Not everyone needs to be an activist for feminism. Perhaps some people don't notice an oppression of women, or perhaps some women simply don't feel oppressed. Perhaps some women fight oppression by simply refusing to be oppressed, by remaining free and independent and autonomous no matter what might be going on around them. In certain cases, activism itself could even be seen as a form of oppression if it involves forcing one's own opinions on another, even when those opinions are that freedom ought to be had by all.

We each must fight for freedom in our own way, as we each have different things to free ourselves from. Each of us have our own struggles and challenges; we cannot expect them to be the same for everyone as they are specific not only to our personalities and to the circumstances of our lives, but also to the vastly different ways in which we each face those circumstances. Artemis can help us see where we are most challenged and inhibited, can show us what restrains us from fulfilling the maximum of our own potential. She can help us exceed those limitations by shedding light on them.

The central focus of the Mounukhia festival remains a celebration of Artemis as light-bringer. When I began my research on Artemis in the ancient world, I quickly discovered that She was not first and foremost the Moon Goddess that so many modern Neo-Pagans claim. Even so, when I went outside to look at the full moon shining silver in the darkness of night, I could feel Her, and sense Her all around me. A Wiccan friend of mine once told me that Selene is the Moon in Heaven, Artemis is the Moon on Earth, and Hecate is the Moon in the Underworld. Something about that saying spoke to me and stuck with me.

Eventually I discovered that the Athenian Mounukhia festival provides us with the only pieces of evidence I know of that directly connect Artemis with the moon,[67] but even these can be somewhat ambiguous. One could argue that offerings of *amphiphontes* to Artemis and the conclusion that it was She Who shone as the full moon on the Athenian navy proves that She had always been a lunar Goddess, and perhaps it was considered too obvious for anyone to bother writing down. On the other hand, one could also argue that because Plutarch had to specify that it was Artemis who shone on the Athenian navy, we can assume that this was not one of Her usual manifestations. It seems there is no way we can know for sure what the ancient Greeks believed, but the lack of any other evidence directly connecting Artemis with the moon leads me to believe that She was not and is not a Moon Goddess.

But then if Artemis is not a Moon Goddess, how could I explain the feelings of Her presence at night under the full moon? Or the sense of Her bow in a slender crescent moon? How could She be the Moon on Earth, a concept that still spoke to me despite everything I learned about how She was not considered to be a Goddess of the Moon in ancient Greece?

The answer to these questions came to me gradually in cumulative glimmers of insight and inspiration. The moon comes to the Earth in the form of moonlight. When I realized this, I began to understand

Artemis's lunar aspect. She is undoubtedly connected to the moon, and suddenly I began to understand how. I have no idea if my conclusion is the same as what the ancient Greeks believed. I know only that it fits with what I know of Her from the ancient world, and it feels true to me.

Artemis is a Goddess of Moonlight. She is not the moon itself, but rather the way its light can illuminate darkness and guide us through it. Artemis can shed light on darkness without destroying it. The light of the Sun is overpowering in its illumination. When it shines, darkness is eliminated. Night ends and day begins. The moon, on the other hand, can bring light into the night without ending it. It can give us just enough illumination to explore the darkness and embrace it for what it is. My limited understanding of Apollo is that He too is not so much a God of the Sun as He is a God of Sunlight, of powerful illumination that drives away all obscurity. Artemis, His twin, is a Goddess of illumination as well, but in a very different way and towards a different purpose.

Even in Her light-bringing aspect, Artemis shows us darkness. The purpose of Her moonlight is to illuminate the night just enough so that we can explore it and navigate it without becoming lost in it. Her light guides us through dark places and dark times that we must pass through and must not ignore, avoid or destroy. She reminds us that the world requires both darkness and light, and shows us how to embrace and understand the darkness around and within us. She can show us the darker parts of ourselves, can illuminate the corners of our soul that we are ashamed or afraid of. She can show us how to come to terms with these pieces, how to accept and embrace all parts of ourselves.

Because the moon is so important to the Mounukhia, there is no set date for the Cataleos Mounukhia festival. In Athens the Mounukhia was always held on the sixteenth of *Mounukhion*, but this was appropriate for a lunar calendar where the sixteenth would always be near the full moon. Choosing a set date on our modern calendar would not necessarily put the festival near the full moon, so instead the official date of the Cataleos Mounukhia is simply the day of the full moon in April.

Celebrating the Mounukhia

To create a Cataleos-style Mounukhia festival, you will need one stick or small branch from an olive or birch tree for each female participant, enough white cotton or wool that each female participant can have enough to wrap their branch, enough clay or other crafting material such that each participant can create a model goat or bear, some portable musical instruments such as drums or recorders, enough clay or other crafting material such that each participant can make their own small model woman, enough string such that each participant can have a sizeable piece, at least two torches or taper candles (if you have a large number of participants you will want more), materials with which to create your own mock naval battle, one small round cake or muffin for each participant, six little birthday candles for each participant, some kind of drink offering, and some divinatory tool. You will also need to find a tree nearby with branches you can reach easily. Choose any tree that you feel is particularly sacred to Artemis or otherwise appropriate for you and your group.

As participants arrive, have them being making their offerings. Each participant will need to make one bear or goat and one model woman. Let people choose if they wish to make a bear or a goat, but explain that the goat appeals to Artemis as a Goddess of sacrifice Who is also merciful, and the bear appeals to Artemis as a Goddess of wild and dangerous things. Explain that the model woman should either represent the participant if she is female, or if the participant is male it should represent some woman in that person's life who they care about and want Artemis to protect. While just about any type of crafting material will work for the bear or goat, you will want something durable for the model women. Polymer clay works well, or you could start with wooden clothespins and have participants decorate and personalize them with paints, yarn, and fabric. Use your imagination, and find something that works with the materials you have available. The model women need be only as complex as you and your group want them to be. If a simple representation such as a small stick with a face painted on it or a vaguely woman-shaped stone sounds appealing to you, then use that instead.

Additionally each female participant will need to prepare a *hiketeria*. Have each woman choose a stick or branch and then wrap it with the wool or cotton. Traditionally these were made with olive branches bound in white wool, but I feel that birch and cotton are also acceptable. Olive was the quintessential sacred tree in ancient Athens, and since I consider birch to be sacred to Artemis, I feel it makes a suitable substitute for olive branches. Cotton is to today's textile industry what wool was to the ancient Greeks, so I feel it is an equally appropriate substance with which to wrap the branches. You may choose to use white wool or cotton yarn or thread, or you could also try loose wool or cotton or strips of white wool or cotton cloth.

Once the offerings are ready, begin with the Cataleos Opening Ritual. Have participants carry their bear or goat with them in the procession, and women should carry their *hiketeria* as well. When the barley prayer is complete, have the acting priest or priestess say another prayer appealing to Artemis the Protectress of Women. Ask the men to stand by quietly and respectfully, lending their supportive cooperation to the women, whose turn it is to act alone. Invite each woman to step forward, one at a time in any order, and say a prayer to Artemis, aloud or silently, asking for Her protection. Explain that when their prayer is done, they should set their *hiketeria* on the shrine or altar as an offering to Artemis given in return for Her protection.

When all the women have said their prayers and given their offerings, have the acting priest or priestess speak a prayer of thanks to Artemis Who watches over all women. Mention in particular one girl whose life was endangered, but was ultimately saved by Artemis' mercy. Tell the story of the foundation of the cult of Artemis at Mounukhia, of the killed bear and of how Embaros promised to sacrifice his daughter to appease Artemis, but then hid her in the sanctuary and sacrificed a goat instead. Then invite each participant to step forward, one at a time in any order, to say their own prayer to Artemis, aloud or silently, and set their bear or goat on the altar or shrine as a gift for Her.

The very first time I put on a Mounukhia festival, I had no particular sentiment in mind for why we should offer bears or goats to Artemis at this point in the ritual. It was simply a commemoration of the myth, and each person was invited to find their own personal message or meaning within it. A very close friend of mine, when it was his turn to dedicate his little bear, said very simply, "Artemis, thanks for accepting the goat." Everyone laughed appreciatively and generally agreed with his sentiment. Since then, that has been the official goat or bear offering prayer for the Cataleos Mounukhia festival. When I have finished telling the foundation myth of the cult at Mounukhia, I say just as simply as my friend once did, "Artemis, thanks for accepting the goat," and then explain how these offerings honor Her as a Goddess who can demand terrible sacrifices, but Who can also be merciful and forgiving when we genuinely put forth our best effort to honor Her well. Embaros did his best to please Artemis by giving Her a valuable offering, but he could not kill his own daughter. Perhaps Artemis was pleased by his devotion to his daughter, or perhaps She simply decided that sacrificing little girls wasn't so great after all. For whatever the reason, She accepted the goat and demanded that from then on the Athenians offer goats and not girls. Whether or not we believe Artemis ever received human sacrifice,[68] now we know that She does not, and we can thank Her for being a Goddess Who is dark and wild and terrifying yet still compassionate towards humankind.

It may seem extremely harsh to envision Artemis as a Goddess so terrible that we must thank Her for not requiring human sacrifice. Remember, however, that She is a Goddess of Nature, of pure wilderness and wild animals. When you think about all the terrible things humans have done and are still doing to the environment, it does not seem so foolish to thank Her for being merciful and forgiving.

Next comes time for the women's dance. Bring your entire group to a place where you have enough room to move around freely. If possible, have this place be near the tree you have chosen. Explain to the participants that women will dance in honor of Artemis to celebrate Her, femininity, sisterhood, and the simple joy of being born a girl. Invite men to participate by providing music. Give them instruments to play, or tell people beforehand to bring instruments for men to use in the ritual. If you don't have any instruments for the men to use, give them a stereo or an mp3 player to use, and have them clap their hands to keep the beat, or even sing along with the music. As for the dance itself, you may wish to teach the women a simple repetitive step for them all to dance in a circle, or you could just let them dance as they please in whatever style they like. Choose whatever methods work best for you and your group.

When the women's dance is complete, tell the participants to take a piece of string and the model woman they made and bring them over to the tree you chose. Have the acting priest or priestess say a prayer appealing to Artemis the Protectress of Women. Mention the music and dance you all created in Her honor, and ask that She give protection to the important women in your lives, whether it be yourself or someone close to you. Instruct each participant to go to the tree, one at a time or all together, and use the piece of string to hang their model woman from one of the branches as they say their own prayer to Artemis, silently or aloud, for whoever they want Artemis to protect.

After the women's dance, gather everyone together for a torch race. Tiki torches are easy to find in the spring and summer, and these can make perfect torches for your race. Alternatively, if you are unable to find or get torches, taper candles can also work. Have the acting priest or priestess say a prayer to Artemis Phosphoros, the Lightbringer, Who in ancient Greece was so frequently depicted as a torch-bearing Goddess. Mention how torches are very much like the moon, in that they too bring light into darkness but do not dispel the darkness entirely, and in that they too can be used to guide people through dark places. Explain that you will race with torches in honor of Artemis.

Divide the participants into at least two teams of at least two people each, and have them run a relay race where one runner passes the torch to the next. They must keep the torch or candle lit as they run, and if it goes out, that runner must relight it and then start their section of the race over again. You can have this set up very simply, where the all the runners being at one point and race to another point and back again before passing the torch to the next runner, or you could have a ring or a trail set up with runners waiting at predetermined points. The larger the teams, the longer the race will last, so keep that in mind when you determine how many teams there will be.

When the race is finished, have the acting priest or priestess say another prayer to Artemis as Phosphoros and Torch-Bearer, proclaiming the race an offering to Her. Name each of the winners, and allow them each a chance to say their own prayer to Her as well if they wish. You may want to have a prize of some kind for the winning team. This could be just about anything you like, and you can choose to either give one prize to the whole team or have a prize for each team member. Wreaths made from birch, olive or some other plant provide graceful, traditional, and inexpensive awards for the winners, but there's certainly precedence for giving gifts to the winners as well. Give the winners the option to keep their prizes, to take their prizes home and dedicate them to Artemis at their own personal shrines, or to dedicate them to Artemis as part of th

-e festival

After the torch race winners have been proclaimed, it's time for your mock sea battle. This too can be as simple or as complex as you like. If you live near the ocean, a lake or pond, or have access to a private pool, you might want to get some inexpensive plastic rafts and water guns or other toy weapons and actually stage or improvise your own mock battle. If you prefer to be less physical, you could let each participant make their own paper boat, raft, or floating craft of some kind and find some way to make a contest or battle out of them. I went this route once with a Cataleos Mounukhia festival, and for the battle we lit each of the boats on fire and sailed them towards one another. The one that burned longest before sinking was the winner. If these activities do not appeal to you, then perhaps a simple game of Battleship will serve as your sea battle. You might devise a way to adapt the game to more than two players or divide the participants into two teams so that each team must make their game play decisions together. Alternatively you might organize a Battleship tournament, having the winners of each match play each other until one person is named the victor. If you decide to arrange your boat fight as a contest, then you might also want to have a prize ready for the winner, and present it in the same way as you did for the torch race. If you happen to live near a harbor of some kind, you might also want to conduct or conclude your boat battle with a prayer asking Artemis to protect it. Explain that you have performed the naval battle or boat contest in Her honor, and hope that in return She will watch over the harbor you live near.

The Cataleos Mounukhia festival is somewhat unique in that it is the only festival where the feast and Theoxenia ritual are not the last activity of the day. While the *amphiphontes* could arguably be dedicated at any time, I've found that the whole experience feels much more intense when performed at night. Thus, after the boat battle, I gather people for the Theoxenia and allow them to relax and feast until it gets dark.

When everyone has finished eating and the sky has grown dark, instruct each participant to take their round cake and stick their six candles in it so that they form a circle. When everyone's *amphiphontes* are ready, gather the participants somewhere outside your ritual space, preferably out of sight of it but still nearby. Have the acting priest or priestess speak a prayer to Artemis of the Moonlight. Explain that one at a time each participant should go into the ritual space alone and dedicate their *amphiphontes* to Artemis with their own private prayer. You may choose to either have a lighter or lit candle ready in the ritual space which participants can use to light their *amphiphontes*, or you may prefer to light the candles in the gathering place and bring them to the ritual space already lit. There are pros and cons to each approach. Processing to the ritual space with the lit cake can be a beautiful experience, but so can lighting the candles in the ritual space in private. You could also let participants choose which approach they prefer. Either way, make sure that participants light their cakes one at a time, either just before they go to the ritual space or when they are in it, as the candles will burn down quickly and each person should be allowed as much time as they like in the space to dedicate their cake alone.

It's also wise to check in on the collection of lit cakes every now and then to see if they have caught fire, and to control the small fires that will inevitably start up. Make sure there is a fire-safe area in the ritual space where participants can leave their cakes. A large oven safe plate or a metal baking pan can each make an excellent surface for leaving the *amphiphontes*. You can usually let cakes burn out safely on a metal pan if they happen to catch fire.

You should also provide participants with some kind of drink offering to give to Artemis along with their *amphiphontes*. Just about any drink can be appropriate, but I like to use white wine, milk, or a light colored juice. You might choose to have a large bottle or pitcher ready in the ritual space from which participants can pour their libation into a libation bowl or onto the ground. Alternatively, you could give each participant their own little container of drink, perhaps in a cup or a small bottle, which they can carry into the ritual space themselves. Choose whichever approach you feel is most fitting for your group.

While each person takes their turn in the ritual space, enjoy the full moon with the rest of the group. If weather permits, go outside and actually look at the moon, enjoy the moonlight and feel Artemis present there. If you are a quiet group, simply be like that and allow each person to have their own internal experiences. If you enjoy conversation, talk about the moon, and have each person share how they feel Artemis's presence beneath it. If the weather obscures the moon, discuss the moon anyway, calling to mind that it is still up there shining down on you, even if you can't see it.

The very last activity of a Cataleos Mounukhia festival is a divination. The Mounukhia celebrates Artemis as an illuminator; thus we take the opportunity to ask Her for guidance and insight. You may choose to begin this while people are going into the ritual space with their *amphiphontes*, having some people waiting in the moonlight while others receive their divination. Having all three activities going on at once will help ensure that no one gets bored, which might be important if your group enjoys fast-paced activities. Other groups may enjoy some quiet time in the moonlight and decide to start divinations after all the *amphiphontes* have been dedicated.

Any type of divinatory tool can work for this activity. This is an entirely modern invention, and there were no ancient methods of specifically Artemisian divination that I know of. The point is to gain insight from Artemis the Guide and Lightbringer. Whichever tool or method you feel best accomplishes that is a good one to use. For Cataleos rituals I use a tool I call the Artemis Oracle. It is a simple divinatory tool I created in which sticks or stones with words written on them are drawn at random and laid out to create some kind of phrase or series of phrases. I offer to help with interpretation if people want it, but usually people prefer to interpret their own results, and I think it's probably best that way. The appendix at the end of this book explains how you can create your own Artemis Oracle if you wish.

When all the *amphiphontes* are dedicated and the divinations are done, you may wish to gather people one last time for a closing prayer and a libation to Artemis, or you may invite people to sit and relax and talk until they are ready to go.

Each year for the Mounukhia I host a candle contest on the Cataleos website so that people who are unable to attend the festival can still participate in some way if they wish. Contestants are invited to create some kind of candle in honor of Artemis. Everyone must start with a simple, solid color candle that is either a taper, pillar, votive or tea light, but from there they can use whatever they like to decorate it. When the candle is finished, they light it up, take a picture, and submit it through the temple email address. All the pictures get posted on the website, and anyone can vote for their favorite entry.

The goal of the modern Mounukhia festival is to help people understand the ways in which Artemis can strengthen each of us and how She can help us understand ourselves and the world around us. Women should get a chance to revel in the camaraderie of sisterhood and feel that their femininity is embraced, honored and supported by the community. All participants should feel encouraged to establish their own connection with Artemis, to discover for themselves the ways in which She can illuminate their lives and their paths.

3: Artemisia

A modern tattoo of Artemis.

The Artemisia as I celebrate it today is an entirely modern invention. While the people of Eretria celebrated a festival of the same name,[69] our modern festival is not based on it. The Cataleos Artemisia festival came about very simply: I decided that the sixth day of the sixth month of our modern calendar ought to be a festival for Her, so I started celebrating one. It began just as a generic celebration of Artemis at which any Artemisian activities were appropriate and welcome, but over time it began to take on a theme. The Artemisia, as it has developed today, is all about sharing and celebrating one's own personal experiences and understandings of Artemis. This is the time to revel in what you have learned about Her from direct interaction, experience, and inspiration.

My personal belief is that research and knowledge of ancient sources should be one half of a modern approach to the ancient Greek Gods. I believe that the other half should be personal experience and modern inspiration and interpretation. I believe that when these two elements work together, each supporting and enriching the other, one can achieve the best and deepest relationship with ancient Gods. I realize that many people may feel differently, and for them perhaps another approach is best. That said, in all my own experiences and to my understanding of those around me, working with ancient and modern in harmony achieves the most profound results.

Sometimes the balancing act between ancient sources and modern ideas can be rather tricky. Since the ancient sources themselves are often contradictory, it can sometimes be difficult to find the meaning beneath all the various versions. A modern idea that at first seems to go against an ancient myth may ultimately turn out to be true to the underlying meaning, or a modern idea that at first seems to fit perfectly with ancient practices may turn out to go against some fundamental concept.

My own desire to make sure that modern ideas always fit with ancient ones is more than just a bias in favor of history. I've simply found that there is invariably insight and wisdom to be gained from knowledge and lore that has survived for thousands of years, whereas my own ideas are relatively young and certainly fallible. Every now and then I may come up with an idea that is absolutely true, and perhaps if I am extremely blessed I will come up with one idea in my entire lifetime that will last as long as the epics of Homer.

All that said, there are many ways in which modern inventions can embellish and enrich a reconstructionist approach to paganism. In some areas knowledge is lost or missing, and modern ideas can fill in the gaps to give us a more complete system to work with. We can make additions that fit with what we know from the ancient world, and that support and enhance our experiences with reconstructed ancient religion. We can discover how the Gods interact with our modern world, and how They manifest Themselves in our own cultural and personal context. Most importantly, through our own modern experiences we bring our religion to life, and make it as much a practical reality as it is an ancient theory.

A Cataleos Artemisia festival should simply be a party. A barbecue or a pot luck picnic would be excellent if weather permits. Provide an environment where people can sit down together, relax, enjoy each other's company, and share what they know about Artemis. Encourage people to talk about their own experiences with Her. If people want to show pictures they made for Her or read poems they wrote about Her, let them do that. If people just want to sit around and talk about Her, that works too. Your group may have some favorite games you want to play or festival activities you want to do, or maybe you just want to go out to dinner somewhere and discuss your interactions with Her. Whatever works best for you and your group is especially appropriate for this festival.

On the Cataleos website I host the Artemisia Anything Contest for people who want to participate in an Artemisia celebration but can't physically attend the festival. Contestants are invited to create something – anything, really – that honors Artemis or expresses their own personal understanding of Her. They send their submissions to the temple email address in some form or another, and anyone can vote on the posted entries.

For all that I am what some people would call a "hardcore recon," I also have some of my own completely modern ideas. Some of the things I thought I came up with myself turned out to be ancient concepts I simply hadn't learned about yet, and maybe more will turn out like that over time, but as of now I still have a few modern ideas that so far I have found no ancient basis for.

I feel that birch trees are sacred to Artemis. Many years ago I read a Neo-Pagan book about trees lent to me by a friend. I can no longer remember its name, but it described silver birch as being "the lady of the wood." Everything the book wrote about birch seemed Artemisian to me, and so I began to consider it Artemis's sacred tree and sacred wood. It also happens to be quite common in New England, whereas olive is rare in our climate. Consequently, whenever a twig or tree branch or a piece of wood or some leaves are called for in Artemisian ritual, I use birch. I also discovered a song by Australian artist Wendy

Rule that refers to Her as "Artemis of the eucalypts,"[70] which I assume refers to the eucalyptus tree. At first I was somewhat skeptical of this association, but now I can easily imagine the eucalyptus groves of Australia being filled with Her presence.

I have felt a connection between Artemis and cats for many years. There is ancient evidence for an association between Her and lions[71], but the domestic cat was not, as far as I know, typically an animal sacred to Her. Nevertheless, the aloof, independent nature of all felines paired with their ruthless efficiency as solitary hunters feels very Artemisian to me. I also feel as though snakes ought to be special to Her, as they are arguably the ultimate efficient hunters.

I know of no confirmed ancient source for a sacred flower of Artemis, so I found one that I felt fit Her. An arguably questionable Neo-Pagan book on herbalism named yellow evening primrose (*Oenothera biennis*) as a hunting flower,[72] and at first this was enough for me to connect it with Artemis. At the time I didn't know that yellow had been sacred to Her in the ancient world, but when I discovered that as well as the fact that yellow evening primrose flowers open in the evening, the choice seemed even more appropriate.

I feel that wildflowers in general are sacred to Artemis, but yellow ones seem to have a particular significance. In New England, yellow flowers are the first to bloom in the spring, and the countryside in Greece was covered with the blooms of *Genista radiata*, a wild European shrub with bright yellow flowers.

I can think of many semiprecious stones that I feel are particularly sacred to Artemis. Clear quartz calls to mind Artemis the Light Bringer, whereas smoky quartz evokes Her darker aspects. Jet can appeal to Artemis as Goddess of Nature, and obsidian, particularly in the form of arrow heads, appeals to the Huntress. Garnet makes me think of the blood of Her prey, so I feel it too is sacred to Artemis the Huntress. Howlite looks to me like it came from the surface of the moon, so I feel that it as well as moonstone can appeal to Artemis's lunar aspects. The rich green of malachite and the earthier shades of jasper make me think of Artemis's connections to the Earth, to nature, and to wild animals.

I think the Gods are so vast that one could make an argument for each color being associated with each of Them. At first, yellow seemed an odd choice of color for Artemis, but the more I think about Her associations with light, childish joy, and the first blooming flowers of spring, the more it makes sense to me. Silver seems an appropriate color for the Goddess of Moonlight, and black seems appropriate for a Goddess so intimately connected with different forms of darkness. The greens and browns of forested wilderness can easily be considered Artemisian, and the purity of white is certainly connected to the Virgin Goddess just as blood red is connected to the Huntress. Gold was frequently associated with many Greek Gods, and blue could easily be connected to Artemis as a Goddess of harbors, a river Goddess,[73] or as the Goddess who stops to bathe in secluded mountain pools.

These are only a few of my own ideas and suspicions, and they only scratch the surface of Artemis's manifestations, gently pointing the way towards deeper concepts and intimate revelations. Think for yourself about Her and what you know of Her, how She appears to you and what you feel is connected to Her, and then consider why those connections might exist, and what that would tell you about Her and about yourself.

4: Kharisteria

The Ancient Festival

Kharisteria roughly translates to "thanksgiving," and this was the central theme of the ancient Athenian festival of that name.[74] It took place on the sixth day of the Athenian month *Boedromion*, and celebrated the Athenians' victory over the Persians at the battle of Marathon.[75] The Athenians, facing impossible odds against the Persian military[76], promised that they would sacrifice to Artemis Agrotera[77] one female goat for each Persian killed. When the battle ended, however, so many Persians had been killed that the victorious Athenians could not find enough goats.[78] Instead they turned the sixth day of *Boedromion* into a festival of Artemis[79] during which they would sacrifice 500 goats to Her ever year in commemoration of the victory She granted them at Marathon.[80] The goats for the sacrifice were lead by *ephebes* in full armor in a military procession to the sanctuary of Artemis Agrotera on the Ilissos.[81]

Artemis was not typically a Goddess of war in Athens,[82] but She did intervene in matters of battle and warfare under certain circumstances.[83] In the case of the battle of Marathon, the Athenians were faced with complete destruction by the Persians if they were not victorious, and so they appealed to Artemis for their survival.[84]

The massive goat sacrifice of the *Kharisteria* was probably not burnt completely as a holocaust. It was most likely offered as a *thusia*,[85] the most common of various types of ancient Greek animal sacrifice. The *thusia* ritual in particular would result in a feast of roasted meat for consumption by the participants.[86]

Thusia has been thoroughly examined by various authors.[87] Participants would bathe, dress in clean clothes, and wear a garland. The animal was adorned and led to the altar, and ideally it went willingly. A maiden carrying a basket full of barley that concealed the sacrificial knife went at the front of the procession, followed by the water bearer. Incense burners and musicians were also commonly part of the procession. Once the procession arrived at the altar, the barley and water were carried around it, the sacrifice, and the participants. Next water was poured over the hands of each participant to cleanse them. Water was also sprinkled on the head of the animal, or the animal was given water to drink. With either of these, the animal would hopefully bow its head in assent to being sacrificed. Each participant would take a handful of barley and hold it while the priest or priestess recited a prayer. When the prayer was complete, the participants all at once would throw their barley at the altar and the sacrifice, as if in confirmation of what the priestess had spoken. Then the sacrificial knife was used to cut some hairs from the animal's forehead, which were burnt in the sacred fire. The animal was then killed with a blow from an axe, and the throat was slit and the blood allowed to spill on the altar, or caught in a bowl and splashed onto the altar. The inner organs, called the *splankhna*, were cooked first and shared amongst the "innermost circle of participants".[88] The bones and inedible parts were burned as an offering to the God or Goddess. The edible meat was cooked and shared with everyone present, although sometimes small portions were burned in the sacrificial fire as well. It was frequently required that all the meat be consumed entirely within the sanctuary, with none taken away or left over. The priestess or the sanctuary would receive the animal's hide.[89] According to the *Odyssey*, a festival would end with the tongue being cut out and cast upon the fire, and then libations being poured into the flames.[90]

The Modern Kharisteria

It took me a very long time to accept the idea that the ancient Greeks performed animal sacrifice. When I first began to study ancient Greek religion, I knew almost nothing about the practice except that it happened, and I wondered how a people could possibly feel motivated to kill animals for their Gods. What would be the point of that? Why would the Gods even want that? It seemed wasteful and barbaric to me, and that nearly turned me away from ancient Greek religion in general.

Then one semester in college I took a class called "Paganism in the Greco-Roman World," which was later renamed to "Religion in the Greco-Roman World." In that class we studied as many forms of ancient Greek religious practices as we had time to cover, and among those was, of course, the act of *thusia*.

As soon as I learned that animal sacrifice was meant to provide food for the community, both the ritual and ancient Greek religion as a whole took on a whole new meaning for me. Parke explains:

> Not only would the worshippers normally have meat when they partook in a festival, but also it would be obviously absurd and wasteful to slaughter an animal on a purely secular occasion. The parts given to the gods did not seriously detract from the value of the meat as food, and those concerned in the slaughtering might as well earn such divine favour as they could. The idea that the gods should show their gratitude to those who regularly sacrificed to them appears already in Homer. Consequently we can picture that even the meat in the butchers' shops had all come from sacrificial victims.[91]

Suddenly it was not the ancient Greeks who appeared barbaric, but our own modern culture instead. The ancient Greeks ate meat from animals that were treated well and killed as humanely as was possible within the technology of the time. The Greeks hoped the animal would go willingly to the sacrifice, and the slaughter was conducted within an honored ritual. The animal was supposed to be at peace with its surroundings up until the very moment of its death; it was not meant to feel stress, anxiety, or suffering. Sacrificial victims were always supposed to be strong, happy, healthy animals, and often creatures meant for sacrifice were never put to work as others might be. Only the best animals could be given to the Gods, and 'best' was judged not only by the creature's physical state, but by its mental and emotional state as well. A creature that had been cared for poorly could not please the Gods.[92]

There are many abhorrent practices in the United States meat industry. These have been thoroughly documented by various sources, and I will not dwell on them here. Many organizations use the horrors of the meat industry to try to convince people to stop eating meat or other animal products and to convert to vegetarianism instead. While I have the utmost respect for individuals who are vegetarians or vegans for this reason, I feel that the conversion attempt is foolish, and at times the way in which it is carried out is downright offensive.

I agree that many farms in the United States ought to be shut down for the way they treat animals. That said, I do not believe that vegetarianism is the answer. For starters, some individuals simply enjoy eating meat, and many, many people will never be swayed to stop consuming it. Furthermore, the human body has evolved on a biological level to be omnivorous. Yes, it is clearly possible to eat a healthy vegetarian diet, but this is not the natural way of our bodies, and many people struggle to get enough of all the nutrients they need as vegetarians. In some parts of the world, it's simply impractical as there is not access to the stunning variety of foods we can get in the United States.

Instead of the radical (and, in my opinion, frequently obnoxious) campaign for vegetarianism and veganism, I choose to support organic, free-range farms. Many people will immediately argue that meat bearing the labels "organic" or "free-range" is not necessarily what it appears to be, but I am certain that there are farms out there who genuinely believe in treating their animals well and providing people with healthy meat and animal products that has come from happy animals. If you are concerned about dishonest labeling, then do some research on local farms or on the brands you have access to, and find out which ones provide products you feel comfortable purchasing.

There are humane farms out there, but right now they are a small minority struggling to compete for business in a world dominated by high-intensity production farms. I think it is a terrible shame that animal rights activists spend so much of their time and energy campaigning for vegetarianism and veganism alone, trying to make humane organic farms look like a fabricated fantasy so that their future converts can't escape to any ideology other than theirs.[93] Imagine what good could be done if all that energy were instead shifted towards promoting and supporting farms that do treat their animals well, with vegetarianism and veganism portrayed as possible options rather than the one and only way. People for whom vegetarianism or veganism is the proper path would still find their way to it, but other people who still want to eat meat might shift to eating organic meat instead. Perhaps with organic farms getting more business and conventional farms getting less, more farms will adopt humane practices. All this would cause a far greater impact than a campaign for vegetarianism alone ever could.

I attempt to live conscientiously within the cycles of nature. I eat meat, but I do what I can to ensure that the meat has come from animals that have been treated well and killed humanely. We cannot (and, in my opinion, should not) deny our own omnivorous instincts, but we must learn to treat the other creatures of this planet with honor and respect. We must attempt to understand them, and to give them the best that we can offer while still remaining true to our own nature. We do not need to change or deny what we are, but rather to be ourselves in balance with everything else.

It is a fact of nature that some animals eat other animals. Some people may argue that with our intelligence as a species we ought to move outside that pattern and cease preying on other creatures. While I can understand this ideology, in my mind plants are just as alive as animals, only they have no mouths with which to cry out when they are cut down, no faces to express their sorrow, no hooves or claws with which to fight back, and so we can too easily forget that even vegetarians and vegans must kill living things and eat them in order to survive. Death feeds life.

This concept is at the heart of the modern Kharisteria. Nothing in this universe can be gained without some kind of sacrifice. Those things that we pay most dearly for are, by definition, the most valuable. That which we suffer to learn we shall never forget. As Burkert says, "Artemis is and remains a Mistress of sacrifices",[94] and at the Kharisteria we celebrate Her as such. At this festival we thank Her for everything that has come at a heavy price or that has been difficult to attain, and we ask for Her help in all our future struggles.

I chose the sixth of September for the official date of the Cataleos Kharisteria. It is usually very close to when the ancient Athenian *Kharisteria* would have been, and I feel that the fall is a fitting time to reflect upon our own personal sacrifices.

Celebrating the Kharisteria

In order to create your own Cataleos-style Kharisteria celebration, you must first decide what kind of sacrifice is appropriate for you and your group. The purpose of a sacrifice in a modern Kharisteria festival is twofold: it serves to thank Artemis for helping us emerge victorious through our own personal struggles, but it is also a way for us to honor the creatures that feed us, be they plant or animal.

It was not unusual in ancient Greece for sacrificial animals to be replaced with animal shaped cakes.[95] You might decide that goat-shaped cookies are the best choice of sacrifice for your group. It's even possible to find goat-shaped cookie cutters if you're not up to shaping the cookies yourself. If you decide to use cookies in your Kharisteria, make enough such that each participant can have one, put them all on plate, and have one person carry them in the procession for the opening ritual. When it comes time for the barley prayer, instead of throwing the barley at the fire and the altar, have everyone throw their barley at the cookies. Then pass the plate of cookies around and have everyone take one. As a preliminary offering, have everyone break a tiny piece of cookie off the head of their goat and toss it into the fire. This, like the lock of hair cut off the animals head, designates the cookie as a sacred offering and makes it fully ready for sacrifice. Say one last prayer giving thanks to the lives of all the plants (and animals if you used eggs in your baking) that were given up to create that cookie, and then all at once have everyone in the group break the necks of their goats. Put the cookie heads into the fire so that Artemis can have Her portion of the sacrifices, and have everyone eat the rest of their cookie. Encourage people to savor their cookies, and to partake in conversation about Artemis while they eat.

If you want to stick with a vegetarian or vegan sacrifice but want something more theatrical than goat-shaped cookies, a loaf of bread can be turned into an effective sacrificial victim. Choose a type of bread that has a relatively stiff crust, and cut a hole in the loaf where the head of the animal will be if you decide to make the loaf look like a creature. Scoop out the soft inside of the bread through that hole, and save it. You must not waste that part of the loaf. Turn it into bread pudding, or eat it as it is as part of the feast, or somehow include it in some other dish. Make certain that it is eaten and not wasted. Fill the hollow loaf with barley, and replace the head. You might want to use toothpicks to make sure the head stays on securely. You can also use other items to decorate your bread sacrifice. Perhaps you want to make it look like a goat, and so you could find little horns to stick onto the head. Or if you're happy having it look just like a loaf of bread, simply put it on a pretty plate and maybe arrange flowers around it. (Some people with sufficient baking skills can actually bake a loaf of bread shaped however they like with the barley already inside it, but this is far beyond my cooking skills.)

When your sacrifice is ready, carry it with you in the opening ritual, and, once again, when it comes time for the barley prayer, throw your barley at the bread rather than at the altar and the fire. Take a small piece off the head or off one end of the loaf and cast it into the fire as a preliminary offering. Then hold the loaf above the altar fire, and with a prayer of thanks to Artemis and to all the living creatures that died to make that bread, stab the loaf and cut through it such that the barley spills onto the fire like blood. If your altar fire is small, you might want to have the barley spill into a bowl instead and place that on the altar. Choose a chunk of bread – perhaps the hole cut when you filled the loaf – to be Artemis's portion and burn it, and then make sure that all of the bread including both the crust and the soft parts you scooped out get eaten. You can save the bread for a feast at the end of the day if you like, or if your loaf is small you can simply eat it right there in the ritual.

If you or the people in your group eat meat, you might want to use this festival as an opportunity to thank the animals that die so that you can live. One way you can do this is by using a piece of meat as your sacrifice and designing your prayers to specifically honor and thank not only the creature that provided your meat, but also all the creatures you have eaten and will eat. I highly recommend you use organic, free range meat for this type of ritual. As with the bread and cookie sacrifices, place your meat on a decorative or decorated plate and carry it with you in the procession for the opening ritual. Throw your barley at the meat, and cut off a tiny portion as a preliminary offering. I generally do not feel that any stabbing or ritual killing is necessary when using a piece of meat for this kind of sacrifice. The animal that the meat used to be was already slaughtered. In this case, the ritual serves to sanctify what has already been done. That said, many people feel like a ritual enactment of the actual slaughter is a poignant way to acknowledge and thus honor the reality of where our meat comes from, so perhaps you will want to include some such dramatization in your ritual. Cut a small piece the meat to be Artemis' portion and burn it in the altar fire, cook up the rest and serve it as part of the feast.

It is still possible to perform *thusia* much like the ancient Greeks did, but this is a massive undertaking that is not for everyone. Many people feel no need or desire to participate in such a rite, and for them any of the other sacrifices can be an equally valuable alternative. However, there are others who feel that in order to eat meat one ought to be able to watch an animal die. Some people feel that a person who can't handle killing an animal should not eat meat at all. For these people, the Kharisteria provides a way for them to acknowledge how a piece of meat gets onto their plate, and allows them to thank not only the creature that dies in their ritual, but also all the other creatures that die for their food.

Aside from providing us with an opportunity to thank the creatures that feed us, a traditional *thusia* can also allow us to take a deep look at our own beliefs about life and death. Raven Kaldera explains:

> Some folks have said that "we no longer need to use killing animals as a sacrifice because we can get meat anywhere and it's not hard to come by anymore." A really good response to that has been "Modern society's attitude towards death is lousy; we're death-phobic. Therefore, being present at a butchering that is done ritually and with sacred intent, the way it should be done, where we can safely struggle with our programmed death-phobia and force ourselves to contemplate death's reality in sacred space, is a worthy sacrifice for modern people."[96]

A properly conducted *thusia* ritual can help us understand the interdependence of life and death, and help us accept our own mortality.

If you and your group decide that you wish to perform your own *thusia*, there are many practical considerations to take into account. First and foremost, consider your motives. Be completely honest with yourself about why you want to attempt the ritual, what you would gain from it, and whether or not this is worth the cost of another being's life. Ask yourself if you could really handle performing such a ritual. It's very easy to talk about, but much more difficult to actually do. If at all possible, go to a local farm and ask to watch one of their slaughters. If you can, volunteer to help with it, and see if you are really up to the task.

I do not wish to encourage every random person to go out and haphazardly attempt their own *thusia* ritual, so I will not discuss any further how to create one. Instead I recommend that people who are determined to perform *thusia* find a local farm that is agreeable to the idea and do it there. Find a farm with knowledgeable staff that is willing to help you make sure that everything is done legally and humanely. If at all possible, contact someone who has done such a ritual before and ask them to help you. Make sure nothing is wasted; all parts of the animal should be eaten, used or offered to Artemis. Don't just go around killing animals without thinking very carefully about all the ramifications of the act. These are living, feeling creatures that deserve our respect and our thanks.

No matter what type of sacrifice you choose to perform for your Kharisteria, the barley prayer will be your opportunity to reflect on the meaning of the act. The barley prayer is more important at the Kharisteria than at any other festival because the central activity of the Kharisteria is the sacrifice, and the barley prayer solidifies its meaning. Some people feel it's silly to recreate a festival that celebrated the victory of one foreign nation over another. In response to this, I often talk briefly during the barley prayer about the meaning of that battle and why it is significant to us. The Athenians weren't just fighting against the Persians. They were fighting to defend their home, their freedom, their way of life, and their lives. Had the Persians been victorious, it would not have meant simply a change in leadership. The entire Athenian people would have been wiped out. The battle of Marathon was a fight for survival, and while we may or may not empathize with the Athenians themselves, we can certainly empathize with the desire to live.

When you make your sacrifice, think about all the things you do to survive. Think about the about the creatures you kill for food, be they plant or animal. Think about the work you do to earn a living. Think about the challenges you have met and suffered through to gain skills or knowledge that allow you succeed. Be thankful for all these things. Thank Artemis that you have it in you to kill so that you can eat, and thank Her for all the times you have struggled to face a challenge and survived.

The type of sacrifice you perform will determine how you organize the rest of your festival, how many other activities you choose to include, and what order you put them in. A cookie sacrifice takes a relatively short amount of time, leaving the rest of the day for whatever games or contests or other activities you want to include. A group that uses a piece of meat for their sacrifice might want to let it marinate and cook while other activities go on, and thus would plan their activities to end when the cooking is done. A *thusia* takes a tremendous amount of time and effort, and the jobs of processing and cooking the meat must be coordinated with whatever other activities you choose to include.

Just about any Artemisian activity can be included in the Kharisteria. Dancing, foot races, and torch races all make good traditional choices, and archery always fits in a festival of Artemis. I feel that war games are also particularly appropriate to the Kharisteria. Perhaps your group will want to stage a mock battle, or come up with some kind of contest involving spears or swords and shields. Perhaps your group would enjoy creating your own armed procession like that of the Athenian *ephebes*, or perhaps a war-themed board game is more your style.

Reciting or enacting myths can also be an engaging festival activity. The myth of Iphigenia's sacrifice is especially appropriate for the Kharisteria, and I prefer the version told in the play *Iphigenia in Aulis* by Euripides. In this play, we discover that Artemis has told Agamemnon to sacrifice his daughter, Iphigenia, to Her so that a good wind will arise, allowing the Greek fleet to sail off to Troy. Agamemnon reluctantly agrees, summons his daughter to the harbor under false pretenses, and then explains the reality of the situation. Iphigenia is initially dismayed, as one might expect, but ultimately accepts her role, not only going to the sacrifice willingly, but also helping to direct it, and doing so with a nobility and composure that comforts her emotionally distraught mother and father. Then, just as she is about to be killed, there is a crash of thunder, and Iphigenia disappears and is mysteriously replaced by a deer which bleeds on the altar in her stead. Everyone realizes that Artemis has carried Iphigenia away somewhere, and accepts the sacrifice of a deer instead.

In another play by Euripides, *Iphigenia in Tauris*, we discover that Iphigenia was swept away to Tauris where strangers are offered in sacrifice to Artemis. Iphigenia's long-lost younger brother, Orestes, has been instructed by an oracle to travel to Tauris to retrieve the sacred image there and give it to the Athenians. Once they realize their kin relationship, Iphigenia and Orestes carry out their task, and as they are fleeing the angry King of Tauris, Athena appears and explains to the g that Orestes is only doing what the Gods told him to do. He lets the brother and sister escape to fulfill the tasks laid out for them in Attica.

This myth teaches us about life, death, and sacrifice on many levels. When Iphigenia is spared, she does not simply disappear, but is replaced by a deer that dies in her stead. Perhaps this can remind us that we are each spared from death by all the plants and animals that die in our place so that we can eat. Iphigenia must lose the family she knows and grow up in a strange land with barbaric customs,[97] all so that she can fulfill a job that Artemis has set out for Her. Ultimately, however, this allows her to return to Greece with incredible prestige to be "...warden of this Goddess's temple around the holy meadows of Brauron." Athena promises Iphigenia she will be buried there and receive offerings at her tomb as a hero would.[98] The statue that Iphigenia and Orestes bring back to Attica will no longer receive human sacrifices, but blood will be drawn from a man's neck and offered to Her instead.[99] Again and again in this myth we see that something is given up in exchange for something else, a cost is paid for any benefit, and although the characters suffer, ultimately they are better off for having survived their challenges.

For those who wish to participate in a community observance of the Kharisteria but can't come to the festival, I host a charity project through the Cataleos website to raise money for Heifer International, an organization that attempts to end hunger through Earth-conscious, animal-friendly projects. Anyone is welcome to participate, but if you would rather host your own charity project, do some research into local organizations that help homeless or needy people in your area, and consider putting on a fundraiser or food drive for them instead.

The point of the Kharisteria is to thank Artemis for everything that comes at a heavy cost and for every victory in our own struggles for survival. At the end of the day, participants should feel a greater awareness of and respect for everything that sustains their lives. They should walk away feeling honored and grateful for everything they have gained from their trials.

5: Elaphebolia

Artemis the Huntress

The Ancient Festival

On the sixth day of their month *Elaphebolion*, the Athenians celebrated a festival in honor of Artemis Elaphebolos, the shooter of deer.[100] Originally the main event of the festival would have been the sacrifice of a stag to Artemis, but in the classical period it became impractical or impossible for people to acquire fresh stags for the event. Instead people offered deer shaped cakes called *elaphoi* ("stags") molded out of honey, dough, and sesame seeds.[101]

While some scholars claim that the *Elaphebolia* became relatively insignificant in later years,[102] I think it is worth noting that the festival was originally important enough that the entire Athenian month *Elaphebolion* was named after it,[103] and even when deer became scarce, the Athenians apparently still found it important to continue honoring Artemis as a deer-shooter.

Xenophon can give us a hint as to why the *Elaphebolia* might have retained its importance despite the decline of deer. He wrote a treatise called *On Hunting* which explains not only the practicalities of how to hunt, but also discusses the virtues of hunting. In fact, the first section of *On Hunting* is entirely devoted to listing various mythological figures, including Asclepios, Odysseus, Nestor, and many more, who were supposedly successful because of what they learned from being hunters. He ends this section by saying:

> These, whom the good love even to this day and the evil envy, were made so perfect through the care they learned of Cheiron [hunting] that, when troubles fell upon any state or any king in Greece, they were composed through their influence;... Therefore I charge the young not to despise hunting or any other schooling. For these are the means by which men become good in war and in all things out of which come excellence in thought and word and deed.[104]

Xenophon then begins the next section with the recommendation that hunting be the first undertaking of a young man before he begins other forms of education.[105] While Xenophon was a Spartan and not an Athenian, we can still guess that hunting had similar value to all ancient Greeks. Therefore, perhaps the educational value of hunting is part of the reason the *Elaphebolia* survived despite the fact that deer became scarce in ancient Athens.

The Modern Elaphebolia

Some people still hunt. Many even do so responsibly, utilizing all parts of the animal they kill. It seems to me that in some communities there is a tendency to despise all hunting based on the abhorrent practices of some. Sadly, I have no knowledge of the actual proportion of respectful hunters to wasteful hunters, but I know that both groups exist in substantial numbers. We should not immediately discredit all hunting just because some people do it wastefully. As with everything else in the world, hunting is not good or bad in and of itself, but rather it can be used well or poorly.

I cannot comprehend the argument that even a well-executed hunt is cruel. A wild animal lives its life in its natural environment, roaming free with its own kind up until the moment of its death. An accurate hunter will kill an animal on the first shot, and even a good hunter with poor aim will swiftly dispatch a dying animal rather than let it suffer. This does not seem so cruel to me. I have already discussed above the necessity of life to feed on death, and it's not like the animal would have lived on immortally if it hadn't been shot. If the animal had been killed in the wild, every piece of it would have gone to use somehow, feeding other creatures in a myriad of ways. The same is still true of an animal brought down by a respectful hunter. Every piece will be used somehow; nothing will be wasted.

It is possible to hunt within the balance of nature, and, in fact, sometimes hunting can be used as a tool to maintain that balance. In the United States, deer populations have exploded due to the decimation of natural predators by various human activities. There exist many attempts to use regulated deer hunting as a way to control the deer population. Not all of these attempts are effective, and there are many controversial debates about why and what can be done, but it is possible to use deer hunting along with reintroduction of natural predators to restore the natural balance of these ecosystems.

While hunting in and of itself is not a bad thing, excessive hunting certainly is, and here we see how the Huntress is also the Protectress of Animals. In order to have creatures to hunt, you must leave enough alive so that they will reproduce and maintain a healthy population. I see this as a particularly important concern in areas of overfishing, where some populations have been so dramatically decreased that whole oceanic ecosystems suffer. In situations such as these, I imagine Poseidon and Artemis both have much to teach us about how to subsist on our environment without depleting it.

Some people have suggested to me that Artemis might now be depicted with a sniper rifle or similar firearm rather than a bow, and while this may sometimes be true, I think there is a very good reason She is still an archer. Humanity has evolved to the point where our technology gives an almost unthinkable advantage over other creatures. While I can certainly see how Artemis as the Goddess Who Never

Misses would manifest with a sniper rifle, the Huntress must exist within a natural balance. The bow is an ancient and primitive weapon that allows a human to hunt but does not put her at such a drastic advantage over her prey.[106] She must still rely on her own strength and skills to track the animal and shoot it accurately. I have experienced firsthand how firearms also require skill to operate effectively, but firing a gun cannot compare to the physical yet intuitive sensation of firing a bow.

Archery is an incredibly enriching activity for hunters and non-hunters alike. To shoot well, one must focus completely on the present, not thinking but simply concentrating with a mental clarity that allows for an intuitive sense of the correct form. One must hold their body in a state of combined exertion and relaxation, aim their shot, and then completely let go. The release itself could be a metaphor for what comes from it. The hand drawing back the string must completely relax for a proper release, not plucking the string but simply letting it go; the hand falling to the shoulder almost mimics the death that flies forth at the tip of the arrow.

One day I thought to myself about how peculiar it is that Artemis would hunt for food since She is a Goddess, and the Greek Gods supposedly eat only ambrosia. First I checked ancient sources to be sure that She did in fact hunt animals for food. In *Hymn III,* Callimachus explains that first Apollo and then Heracles would take the animals Artemis hunted when She came to Zeus's palace, saying that Heracles would be "waiting to see if [Artemis] will come home with some fat meat." The impression given is certainly one that the animals would be butchered and the meat would be eaten. Thus it is somehow significant, even if only metaphorically, that the animals Artemis hunts would be consumed.

I think that significance is twofold. First, as a Goddess of Nature, Artemis must exist within the natural laws of conservation. Nothing is wasted in nature. Everything goes to some use, be it through consumption or decomposition or any other means. Somehow everything always ultimately feeds everything else. Therefore the animals She hunts must also feed something. In celebrating this aspect of Artemis we can acknowledge how we are interconnected with everything else on this earth. Secondly, Artemis as the Huntress is also a Goddess of self-sufficiency. A hunter can go out and find her own food, and does not need to depend on anyone else for sustenance. Here we find another way that modern people can identify with a Hunting Goddess: she helps us not only with our own personal hunts in whatever forms they might take, but She can also help us to be independent and self-sufficient individuals.

The ancient Athenian *Elaphebolia* was celebrated in early spring, but in the United States deer hunting is illegal in the spring. It seems silly to me to celebrate the Deer Huntress when it's illegal to hunt deer, so I moved the date of the modern festival to October 6th, which falls in or near most modern deer hunting seasons.[107]

Celebrating the Elaphebolia

In order to create your own Cataleos Elaphebolia festival, you will need enough crafting materials such that each participant can make their own small model bow and arrow, materials for a group hunt, enough crafting materials such that each person can make small model animals, a piece of string for each participant to use to hang their model animal, a deer-shaped cake for each participant, enough crafting materials such that each person can create a symbol of what they hunt for, and, if possible, the space and materials for an archery contest and a prize for the winner. You will also need to find a tree with branches low enough that the model animals can be hung from them.

You will probably want to have the deer cakes baked ahead of time. There are many possible recipes you can use, but since I am not an exceptional baker, I usually use sugar cookies cut with deer-shaped cookie cutters, and when they are done baking I glaze them with honey and sprinkle sesame seeds on top.

As participants arrive, have them make their model bows, arrows, animals and hunting symbols. The bows and arrows can be made from any material you like, but I've found that bamboo cooking skewers work well for both bows and arrows, and thick thread such as upholstery thread can be used for a bowstring. You can cut up craft feathers and glue them to the blunt end of skewers to make arrows, or even use bits of paper for fletching instead. The model animals should be made of some kind of sturdy material just like the model women for the Mounukhia, and they should depict any animal that is hunted or raised for food. If your group is particularly craft-challenged, you could even consider using Christmas tree ornaments shaped like animals. The hunting symbols can be as simple or as complicated as you like. These should represent anything that you are trying to accomplish or attain: perhaps a new house or apartment, or a better job, a college degree, or even something small like the perfect couch to go with your living room. Anything at all that you personally want Artemis's help in hunting for should be represented in your symbol. You can choose to have participants make complex models of what they want to hunt for, or you could have participants simply draw a picture of what they want on a piece of paper. Feel free to be as creative or simplistic with that as you like.

When everything and everyone is ready, gather for the opening ritual and have each participant carry their tiny bow and arrow in the procession. After the barley prayer, have the acting priest or priestess say a prayer to Artemis the Huntress, asking Her to help us understand what weapons and tools we each have that we can use on our own personal hunts, and asking Her to help us each become the best hunters we can be. Ask Her to aid us in becoming strong, independent, and self sufficient. Invite each participant to step forward one at a time and say their own prayer to Artemis, aloud or silently, asking for Her aid and instruction. As each participant finishes their prayer, they should offer their bow and arrow to Artemis as a gift in return for Her assistance.

Once everyone has dedicated their bow and arrow, it's time to enjoy your own hunt in celebration of the Huntress. There are infinite ways to arrange this activity. Perhaps you want to model your hunt after an Easter egg hunt: get a bunch of inexpensive model animals – most craft stores and toy stores sell packages of tiny plastic animals – and hide them all around your festival area. Give each participant a basket, and tell them to collect as many little animals as they can find. Perhaps you would rather organize your hunt as a scavenger hunt. Write up a list of items for your participants to find, give them a certain amount of time, and send them off to get as many as they can. You can divide the participants into teams if you like, or just each person off on their own. You could create a hunt by taking one special item or stuffed animal and hiding it somewhere, then leaving a trail of clues for the group to follow to find it. Perhaps the clues will be reminiscent of tracking an animal through the woods, or perhaps each clue will be a puzzle that the participants must solve together to find the next clue, or you could divide participants into two teams, and leave two copies of each puzzle at each clue, and make it a race to see who can get to the prey fastest. If you choose any of these methods that turns the hunt into a competition, you should consider having some kind of prize for the winner or the winning team, which could be as simple as a wreath of birch or olive for them to wear. You might instead want to arrange your hunt as a series of puzzle clues that lead to a safe spot, or to a doorway that symbolizes escape into the forest. Have one team be the prey and one team the hunters. Allow the prey team to start the puzzles first, then let the hunters begin and see if they can catch up to the prey team before the prey get to the safe spot. If your group is especially physical, you might want to simply let the participants decide if they want to be prey or hunters, then let the prey run off, give them a head start, and then challenge the hunters to go bring back one of the prey people. If you decide to do this, make sure you have enough space to carry it out effectively, and make sure to take a few safety precautions. Of course, if your group is so inclined, you might just want to go out and hunt deer.

When your hunt is finished, gather the participants together and allow everyone a few moments to reflect on the activity, to sense Artemis's presence, and to think about what they might have learned from the activity. If you used special tools in your hunting, such as baskets to gather the little animals or the list of items for the scavenger hunt, you might want to consider dedicating those to Artemis.

After everyone has had a little time to reflect on the hunt, allow everyone to get their personal hunting symbols, then gather again and have the acting priest or priestess say a prayer to the Huntress. Ask Her to help us attain the various things we each hunt for in our lives. Invite each participant to step forward and say their own prayer to Artemis, aloud or silently, and dedicate their personal hunt symbol to Her.

Once everyone has dedicated their symbols to Artemis, it's time for a presentation of the myth of Aktaion. As usual, this can be a simple recitation or a full blown dramatization depending on what would be best for your group. As with all myths, are a few different versions of the story of Aktaion, but the one I like best goes as follows: Aktaion was a competent hunter, but one day he accidentally gazed upon Artemis bathing in the forest. She turned him into a deer, and drove his hunting hounds into a frenzy so that they ate him.[108] The various alternate versions of this myth give different reasons for how Aktaion came to see Artemis bathing, what his intentions were, and why Artemis turned him into a deer, but in all these versions the hunter Aktaion takes on the appearance of a deer and is devoured by his own hunting dogs. This myth shows how fine the line can be between predator and prey, and teaches us all to be careful and respectful hunters.[109] At any moment we could become the hunted instead and find ourselves wishing that the ones hunting us are similarly honorable.

When your presentation of the Aktaion myth is complete, have each participant get their model animal and a piece of string to hang it with and gather around the tree you have chosen. Have the acting priest or priestess say a prayer to Artemis Potnia Theron, the Mistress of Animals, asking Her to protect the animals that we kill for food so there will always be a surviving healthy population. Even if your group does not eat meat, you can still ask Artemis to watch out for the animals that other people hunt, making sure that enough escape so that there will always be more, and you can ask Artemis to watch over farms to be sure that domestic food animals are well cared for. Allow each participant to hang their model animal on the tree, one at a time if you prefer, and say their own prayer to Artemis.

The next activity should be your archery contest. Remember that bows and arrows are real weapons, and can cause serious injury or death if used improperly or disrespectfully. If you can hold a real archery contest, by all means do so, but do it safely. Take your group to a local archery range, or make sure you have a licensed archery coach present to keep all your participants safe. If you don't have access to real bows and arrows (remember that many archery ranges have inexpensive equipment to rent), then consider using toy bows and arrows for a contest instead. When the contest is complete, gather everyone together and have the acting priest or priestess say a prayer to Artemis the Archer. Name the winner of the contest and give them the prize, and allow him or her to say their own prayer to Artemis.

Next have the participants each take a deer-shaped cake and gather once again in the ritual space. Have the acting priest or priestess say a prayer to Artemis Elaphebolos, the Shooter of Deer. Mention how the Deer Huntress is still important to your group, whether it be because you wish Her to literally help with deer hunting, or because you want Her blessing with other activities that also possess the essence of the deer hunt. From here you can choose to either have each person step forward individually to offer their deer cake to Artemis with a prayer, or your group could break the necks of the deer together, offer the heads to Artemis and eat the rest, as with the goat shaped cake option for the Kharisteria. It is likely that the deer of the ancient Athenian *Elaphebolia* would have been offered in a *thusia*, so it is perfectly appropriate to offer a portion of the cakes to Artemis and eat the rest.

If your group eats meat, you might consider including venison or other types of game meat in your Theoxenia feast. One year I was organizing an Elaphebolia ritual at my friend's house in Rhode Island, and we wanted to have venison for our feast. Unfortunately, the deli where we had planned to get our venison had shut down, so we ended up having to go to a regular grocery market to get meat for the feast.

We were somewhat disappointed, but I simply said that if Artemis really wanted us to eat venison at Her festival, She could provide us with a way to obtain it. We went into the store, and not ten minutes later a package of venison literally fell off the shelf in the meat section just as I was walking past it.

For people who are unable to come to the Cataleos Elaphebolia festival but still want to participate in an Elaphebolia celebration, I host a photo hunt through the Cataleos website. People are encouraged to go out and enjoy the wilderness and take a picture of any wild animal they see. Each person gets to submit one photo to the contest, and everyone can vote on which entry is the best.

The Elaphebolia helps us to understand the hunter within us. We all possess the instincts of pursuit, and with Artemis's help we can learn to embrace and understand our own drive to hunt, and become more respectful and more effective hunters.

6: Theronia

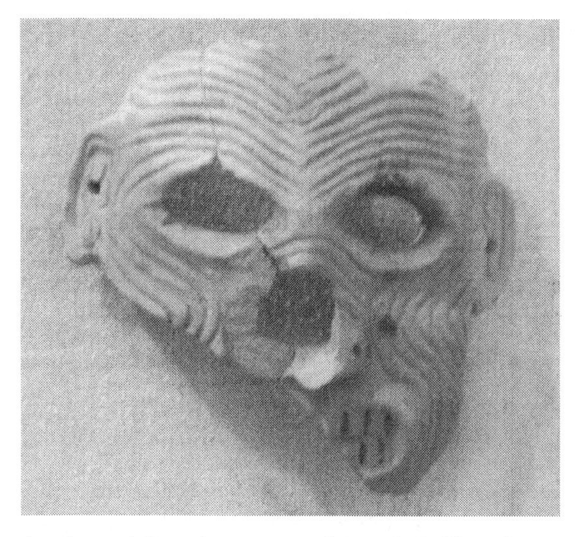

A votive mask from the sanctuary of Artemis Orthia at Sparta. (Archaeological Museum of Sparta)

The Ancient Festival

There was no ancient festival I know of called Theronia, but I included some elements of the Spartan cult of Artemis Orthia when I created the Theronia we celebrate today. Potnia Theron, the Mistress of Animals or Lady of Beasts, was undoubtedly worshipped at shrines of Orthia, and "was popularly identified at Sparta with Artemis from an early period."[110]

Many dances were performed in honor of Artemis Orthia at Sparta. Among these was the *morphasmos*, in which dancers would mimic the actions of all kinds of animals.[111] Masks were worn during other dances, and they portrayed terrifying gorgons, grotesque lepers, old women, and inspiring warriors.[112] These masks were possibly worn by young men during rites of passage in order to allow them to experience multiple different states before becoming the model citizens they were expected to be. Vernant explains:

> At the sanctuary of Artemis, the youths who put on masks to perform their dances and songs were not only selecting the figure of the accomplished warrior who, with his manly courage, constituted the ideal of the *agoge.* They also tried on different forms of alterity so as to exorcise them through the mimicry of ritual.[113]

The Modern Theronia

The idea for the Theronia festival originally arose from a modern need. At the time I kept many snakes as pets and had a number of friends who had snakes as well. For many species of snake in captivity in the Northeast, the dry, cold winter can be a dangerous time of year. Extra vigilance is required to make sure that pet reptiles have enough heat and humidity. I thought it would be prudent to create a festival for Artemis sometime in the beginning of winter that would ask for Her protection for these animals. I considered the fact that Artemis had both horses[114] and hounds to be proof enough that She is a Goddess of pets as well as feral creatures, and thus I created the Theronia to be celebrated in honor of Her on December sixth.

Almost immediately this idea began to expand. The festival became a celebration of Artemis Potnia Theron, the Mistress of Animals, and people would request Her protection for all the world's creatures, wild and domestic. However, just as in the Elaphebolia, where the Protectress of Animals is never far removed from the Huntress, in the Theronia we are reminded that Potnia Theron not only protects animals but also hunts them. The winged image of Artemis Potnia Theron[115] holds an animal in each hand, and most often they are held by the neck, as one would hold captured prey rather than a companion animal.

With this the Theronia takes on a darker theme. The Mistress of Animals is also the Lady of Beasts. She protects not only the fragile fawn but also the deadly wolf that hunts it. Nature has no sense of good and bad or right and wrong. There are no animals that are more or less innocent than any others; each creature functions only as its instincts deem it must. Each animal performs its own necessary role, acting within the balance of its ecosystem. It is only humans who have attempted to create rules of ethics and morality to guide our behavior.

Beneath these social constructs that shape our behavior, we still have within us a feral beast. We see the beast reveal itself a little whenever we let loose in a destructive task, lose our temper, or engage in any sort of combat. If we suppress this beast and keep it always chained down in the dark depths of ourselves, then on those occasions when it does pop out, it will do so with an unbridled rage. At the Theronia, Artemis shows us how to embrace our inner beast, bring it to the surface, and give it some exercise. This can give us a better understanding and acceptance of the darker parts of ourselves, such that we can manage them better in our daily lives and perhaps even learn to use them as helpful tools, or integrate them into the whole of our identity.

Celebrating the Theronia

To create your own Cataleos-style Theronia festival, you will need enough craft supplies such that each participant will be able to make one mask and some models or representations of animals, a piñata shaped like some kind of prey animal, a bat or stick with which to beat the piñata, and some music and a space for a beastly dance.

When participants arrive, have them begin making their masks and models. There are many options of methods of mask construction. If your group is particularly ambitious, you may want to make casts of each others' faces and then each person can decorate an exact cast of their own face. If you want a somewhat simpler project, plain basic masks are available at most craft stores, or you could use construction paper or paper plates to create your masks. Either way, each participant should decorate their own mask to display the beast within themselves. The idea is to take the thing that we usually keep buried down within and for once wear it on the surface instead. The representations of animals can be as complex as detailed clay models or as simple as drawings on a piece of paper or index cards. One year my group made animals out of the colorful fuzzy pipe cleaners available at most craft stores. Allow each participant to make as many animals as they want.

When the masks and animals are ready, gather everyone for the opening procession, and have each participant carry with them the animals they made. When the barley prayer is complete, have the acting priest or priestess appeal to Artemis Potnia Theron as the protectress of animals. Ask Her to protect the world's creatures through the coming winter, and explain that you have made gifts to give in return for Her protection. Invite each participant to step forward and dedicate their model animals to Artemis with their own prayer to Her, spoken aloud or silently as they see fit. Encourage people to explain why they made the particular animals they did, but do not require it.

When all the animals have been dedicated, have the acting priest or priestess once again appeal to Artemis Potnia Theron, only this time as the Lady of Beasts. Ask Her to help you see and embrace and the beast within. Instruct your participants to put on their masks and feel their beasts coming near to the surface. Then bring your group to the space you have cleared, play your music, and begin your dance.

Your masked dance can take on whatever form you like. If you prefer to be especially traditional, you could mimic the actions of particular animals and allow those movements to awaken the animalistic instincts within yourself. If your group prefers to be more spontaneous, you could simply allow participants to move in whatever way inspires them. Pick a piece of music that is appropriate both for the tastes of your group and for the purpose of the activity. The dance should raise your own beastly energies and bring your inner predator to the surface.

When your dance is finished, it's time to channel those primal energies into the destruction of your piñata. The idea for a Theronia piñata came one day when my group had no space for a proper beast dance. We still wanted to do something that would give our inner beasts a little exercise, so we took stock of the materials we had on hand, and someone suggested a piñata. We cut and taped pieces of paper into the shape of a rabbit and filled it with candy someone just happened to have with them. Then we bound a bunch of birch branches together to make a thick stick to use as a bat and took turns taking a swing at our homemade rabbit piñata. You do not need to make your own Theronia piñata unless you feel particularly motivated to do so. A store bought piñata will work just as well, and you could even modify a bought piñata to be particularly appropriate for your group. It's entirely appropriate to fill the piñata with some kind of edibles that your group can share and even later include in your Theoxenia feast. Any bat or stick can be used to beat your piñata – we used a bundle of birch branches only because that's what he happened to have on hand – or you could even use your bare hands if your group feels particularly brutal. You may choose to blindfold each participant as they take their turn so that they must use their animal instincts to find the prey, but if you do so make sure that everyone (and everything) else is a safe distance away. You could allow one person to hold the rope suspending the piñata and let them pull it higher or drop it lower as each person tries to attack it, just as a prey animal would struggle to evade its predators. Alternatively you may just want to let each participant take one swing at the piñata, channeling all their beastly rage into it, until someone finally busts it open (although if you choose this last option be sure that your piñata is strong enough to allow each participant to have at least one turn). You might even encourage participants to rush to the fallen piñata in a frenzy, just as children do to grab their share of the candy, or as lions do when a lioness brings down a gazelle.

When your piñata has been destroyed and its innards have been divided among the group, have the acting priest or priestess say another prayer to Artemis the Mistress of Beasts, thanking Her for helping you to understand and embrace the beasts within yourselves. If your piñata was constructed from safely combustible materials, you may wish to burn what remains of it as an offering to Her. Instruct participants to remove their beastly masks, asking that Artemis help your remember all that you have learned throughout the festival. Ask that even though you now return to controlled, civilize life, you may always remember the beast within. Ask Her to help you learn to work with your beast as an ally, or to utilize those beastly energies that are a part of your whole self. Allow participants the option of dedicating their masks to Her or keeping them for themselves.

For people who are unable to attend the Cataleos Theronia festival but still want to participate in the celebration, I host the Theronia Inner Beast Contest through the Cataleos website. Contestants may submit any piece of their own art, music or writing that expresses their inner beast. Entries are posted on the site, and anyone can vote for their favorite one.

The Theronia should remind all of us that we too are animals. Like the Arkteia, the Theronia shows us that despite the societal customs that constrict our behavior, deep within we are beasts of the wild. When we pray for Her to protect animals, we also pray for Her to protect us, and to help us understand and embrace the animals within us, so that we too can live within the chaotically ordered cycles and recombinant harmonies of Nature.

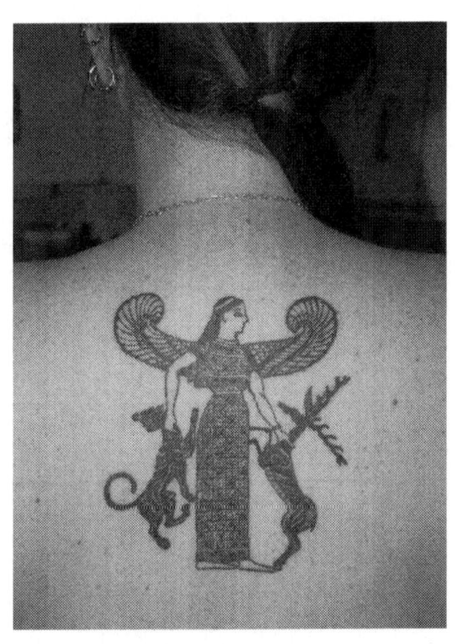

Artemis Potnia Theron

Joint Festivals

The Thargelia and Philokhoria differ from the festivals I have discussed thus far in that they each celebrate more than one deity. Consequently, there are certain changes you may wish to consider. Because each of these festivals primarily honor both Artemis and Apollo, you should consider having both an acting priest and priestess to conduct the various activities. While the gender of the acting priest or priestess has not been of terribly great importance up to this point, you may wish to have a male and female pair acting for the Thargelia and Philokhoria. There is a certain energetic duality and polarity present with the Twins, and a priest and priestess can often (but certainly not always) articulate this more clearly than a pair of priests or a pair of priestesses.

You should also consider addressing all the deities involved in each festival in your initial barley prayer; at the very least you should mention both Apollo and Artemis. Similarly, your Theoxenia should include all the deities involved in the festival. Generally speaking, it is a good idea to include the same deities in your Theoxenia as you mention in your barley prayer, but since the Thargelia follows a relatively unusual format, you may decide to do differently there.

7: Thargelia

Artemis pouring a libation into a bowl held by Apollo. (Archaeological Museum of Sparta)

The Ancient Festival

The Athenian festival *Thargelia* took place on the sixth and seventh days of their month *Thargelion*,[116] but there was probably some type of *Thargelia*-like festival celebrated all over the Ionian states at roughly the same time.[117] At Delos this would have been a conjoint festival of Artemis and Apollo, but in Athens it became primarily a festival of Apollo.[118]

The first day of the *Thargelia* was devoted to purification. In Athens this was accomplished by a ritual involving *Pharmakoi*, individuals chosen to represent the rest of the population. Two ugly, poor men were selected, one representing all the women of Athens and the other representing all the men. They were "fed for some time at the state's expense,"[119] paraded around the city, then beaten with fig branches, pelted with squills (sea onions), and ultimately driven out or exiled. These individuals were meant to be scapegoats for the entire community, and when they were driven out, all impurities went with them.[120] On the second day of the ancient Thargelia, first fruit offerings were given to Apollo in the form of a *thargelos*. This was a pot or stew filled with all kinds of boiled vegetables, which was offered to Apollo at His sanctuary.[121]

Chrimes points out the likely connection between the Athenian Thargelia and the Spartan festival of Artemis Orthia during which young men were whipped at Her altar. He gives a detailed analysis of the similarities between the two festivals, and suggests that the whipping of the *epheboi* may have originally served to purify the entire Spartan community.[122]

At Delos, the sixth and seventh of *Thargelion* were thought to have been the birthdays of Apollo and Artemis respectively.[123] Presumably they had a festival for the Twins on those days, and there was at least one festival of Artemis and Apollo held on Delos to which the Athenians would send an official delegation.[124]

The Modern Thargelia

My friend and I often comment that we always feel a deep need for a Thargelia festival as soon as the time comes for it, although perhaps this is nothing more than the seemingly universal human need for spring cleaning. I imagine much has already been said in other places about the value and necessity of spring cleaning and cleansing in a Neo-Pagan context, so I will not dwell on it here. Many Hellenistai celebrate the Thargelia as a festival of Apollo alone, but since the festival originated as a joint celebration in honor of the Twins, I have chosen to bring it back in this direction for the Cataleos festival calendar. However, instead of having Artemis preside over the purification and Apollo over the first fruits offering as was done originally with the ancient Thargelia, I have found that a modern festival works best with both deities being involved in all the activities.

While it was the sixth and seventh days of *Thargelion* that were thought to be the birthdays of Apollo and Artemis, I believe more importance lies in the number of the days than in the precise days themselves. I wanted to include birthday elements in the Cataleos Thargelia, and so I chose the sixth and seventh of May as dates for the modern festival. That said, a two-day-long celebration is not strictly necessary for the Thargelia, and is in fact likely to be relatively uncommon. The festival is designed to take place all in one day, but if you find that a two day celebration is practical for your group, there are many ways you could divide and enhance the festival activities.

Artemis and Apollo. (Archaeological Museum of Delphi)

Celebrating the Thargelia

To create a Cataleos-style Thargelia ritual you will need cleaning materials practical for your space, a method by which each participant can perform their own purification, a doll or human-shaped figure to use as a *pharmakos*, a vegetable dish to serve as a *thargelos*, a meat dish or reasonable substitute, a loaf of bread, and a birthday cake for Apollo and Artemis. If your group enjoys arts and crafts activities, then you might also want to create small birthday gifts for Artemis, Apollo and Leto. These should be prepared when the participants first arrive, and can be whatever type of offering you like. A bow and arrow or a stag are suitable for Artemis, a lyre or a tripod would be good for Apollo, and palm trees are especially appropriate for Leto, as She supposedly braced Herself against a palm while giving birth.[125]

The *thargelos*, meat dish, and loaf of bread should also be prepared ahead of time. The *thargelos* could be any vegetable dish that you are willing to offer to Apollo. If you are particularly ambitious you may want to track down a traditional recipe for Greek boiled vegetables, but a simple dish of steamed vegetables perhaps seasoned with bay can work just as well, as can a vegetable stew of your own design. A food offering for Artemis will ideally consist of some kind of meat, and this can be of any type and cooked in whatever way your group prefers. If your group does not eat meat, then consider substituting whatever kind of food you most often use as your primary protein source. Alternatively, if you do not eat meat but feel that there is some other type of food that is particularly Artemisian, use that instead. The loaf of bread will be an offering for all the other Gods, so whether you choose to bake one yourself or buy one from your local bakery or grocery market, be sure that it is of a suitable quality.

Unlike other festivals, the Thargelia ought not to start immediately with the opening ritual. Instead, it begins with three phases of purification: purification of space, purification of self, and purification of the community. When all the participants have arrived, gather everyone together and have the acting priest and priestess say a brief opening prayer to Apollo and Artemis. Ask for Their help to purify your space, yourselves, and your group so that you can be made ready for the coming bounty of spring. Then pass out the cleaning supplies and have everyone clean a bit. This can be as intense or as simplified as you feel is appropriate for your space. If you are outdoors, perhaps ritual sweeping and smudging would be sufficient; simply pass the broom and the smudge stick among the group so that everyone gets a chance to participate. If you are indoors, don't hesitate to use modern cleaning supplies if you feel they are appropriate or necessary. However you choose to organize this activity, be sure that everyone at least gets the chance to feel that they have participated in a group cleaning effort, but don't make anyone feel that you made them clean your house for you.

Once you have appropriately purified your space, it's time for personal purification. Each individual will have their own particular tastes for purification rites, even within an established group. For some people, a quiet moment with some cleansing incense will be the perfect way to cast out their internal clutter. For others, ritual scourging is the best way to cleanse spirit and soul. In order to make this part of the festival easily personalized for each participant, prepare an empty room or secluded space in which participants can go to purify themselves. Have a variety of purification tools available there for people to use. Some items you might consider are smudge sticks, incense, a fan, salt, water, soap, a scourge, a music player of some kind with a variety of music for people to choose from, or any other purification tools that you or your group prefers. Allow each participant to take a turn alone in this space and perform whatever rites of purification they feel is necessary. Encourage them to say their own prayers to Artemis and Apollo, first requesting Their assistance and then thanking Them for it.

If you work with a consistent, tightly knit group, you may find that creating your own ordeal ritual similar to that held in honor of Artemis Orthia will provide an intensely purifying experience. In the modern day, however, such rites are rarely appropriate for casual groups where membership and attendance is more fluid, and are generally a bad idea for public ritual.

When each person has purified themselves to their content, gather the group together again to create or personalize your *pharmakos*. While the individual purification allows each participant to get rid of their own personal impurities, the *pharmakos* is meant to purify the community as a single entity. It does not focus on what each person wishes to be rid of, but instead take with it the *miasma* of the whole group. Just about any vaguely human shaped figure can be used as a *pharmakos*, or if some other creature or symbol is particularly appropriate to your group, that could work as well. Some people might like to create a *pharmakos* out of straw or grass, while others might want to use a doll that they purchased. Gather around your *pharmakos* and take time to talk with your community about everything you want to be rid of. Think of all the drama you want to leave behind, or any negativity within your group that you wish to cast away. Have some method by which your participants can add their own personal touches to the *pharmakos*. If you're using a doll you purchased, then perhaps you will have special clothing to dress it up in, or you could give each participant a marker with which to write or draw their own symbols on the doll or its clothing. If you made a figure out of grass or straw, then perhaps you could give each participant a piece of paper on which to write what they wish to add to the *pharmakos*, and then these messages could be woven into the straw. For any type of figure you could use a cloth to make a shroud, and let each participant write messages or symbols on the shroud.

When the *pharmakos* is ready and has been charged with all the things your group wants to be rid of, find some way to destroy it. Perhaps you will first want to throw stones at the figure or beat it with sticks to encourage all you're casting out to flee and stay distant. If you've made your *pharmakos* out of straw or grass or some other safely flammable material, then perhaps you will want to burn it. If your *pharmakos* is not safely flammable, then burying it or breaking it and then burying the pieces will work just as well. Whatever method you choose, be sure that everyone can participate in some way, and that nothing is left of your *pharmakos* when the rite is complete.

Now that you and your group have been thoroughly purified, it's time to give first fruits offerings to Apollo, Artemis, and the rest of the Gods. Gather the participants with a procession choosing three people to carry the *thargelos*, the offering for Artemis, and the loaf of bread, and begin what would otherwise be the Cataleos opening ritual. When the barley prayer is finished, have the acting priest and priestess step forward and offer first the *thargelos* to Apollo, then the meat offering to Artemis, and then the loaf of bread to the rest of the Gods, saying a separate prayer with each offering. If your group feels particularly close to agricultural cycles, then perhaps your prayers can focus on the first fruits offerings as an advanced thanks for all the food you hope to receive in the coming season. If you or any of your participants have your own farms or gardens that yield products in spring, then perhaps you might want to contribute a portion of the year's first harvest to the first fruits offerings. This would be done with the hope that, in return for your gratitude towards Them, the Gods will then bless you with a more bountiful harvest throughout the rest of the year. If you feel more inspired by the many other ways that the Gods bring new things into our lives, then you could instead think of the first fruits offerings as a symbol of thanks for all the good that you hope the coming year will bring. Feel free to include any Gods you like in the bread offering, and not just Gods of the Greek pantheon. If there are any Gods that you and your group feel particularly close to, you may wish to mention Them by name, but make sure that the offering is given to all the other Gods as well, if only by saying exactly that.

It is up to you to decide whether you want to give the entirety of your first fruits offerings to the Gods or whether you want to have some of those foods as part of your Theoxenia feast as well. You may decide to make your *thargelos*, meat offering, and bread offering in large portions such that the first serving of each can be given as first fruits and the rest can be shared in the feast, or you might want to make smaller portions and give them all completely to the Gods.

The Theoxenia feast at the Thargelia can be a much more ritualized occasion than normal. To begin with, three extra places should be set at the table: one for Artemis, one for Apollo, and one for Their mother, Leto. Each of these Gods should be officially welcomed to the feast with their own prayer. Artemis and Apollo should be invited as the guests of honor since the feast is also Their birthday party. Leto should be invited to celebrate the birthday of Her children, and honored as the divine mother who bore such wonderful offspring. If you decided to make gifts for Artemis, Apollo and Leto, then this would be the time allow each participant one at a time to give their gifts to each of Them, setting each offering next to the plate of the appropriate deity and adding their own prayers if they so desire. Once the gifts have all been given out, let everyone enjoy the feast and celebrate the birth of the Twins. Make sure to give at least a small portion of each dish to all three of the divine guests.

When the feasting is just beginning to wind down, it's time to bring out the cake. You might decide to have one cake for both Artemis and Apollo, or get a pair of small cakes and give one to each of Them. If you or someone in your group enjoys baking, you could make the cake or cakes yourself, but for the baking-challenged a store bought cake could easily be personalized with a little decorative frosting. You may want to design your own special birthday ritual to perform along with presenting the cake, but I've found that simply singing "Happy Birthday" to Them and letting the acting priest and priestess blow out the candles on Their behalf works perfectly well.

At the end of the Thargelia, participants should feel cleansed, refreshed and renewed. The festival helps us to dust off our lives and get rid of all the things that plague and hinder us, so that we can make room for new growth and development. The Thargelia can also help us cleanse our communities, getting rid of the old grudges that lead to arguments, and making room for new bonds. The festival should leave everyone feeling excited and hopeful over the fresh potential of a new year.

8: Philokhoria

From left to right: Zeus, Leto, Apollo, and Artemis. (Archaeological Museum of Vravrona)

There was no ancient festival called the Philokhoria, and I did not knowingly borrow from any specific ancient festivals or rituals. I invented the whole concept, but my inspiration came from a pair of ancient hymns. The idea first occurred to me when I read through Callimachus' hymn to Artemis. There was one tiny passage that jumped out at me as festival material:

> But when the nymphs encircle thee [Artemis] in dance... the god Helios never passes by that beauteous dance, but stays his car to gaze upon the sight, and the lights of day are lengthened.[126]

I had heard many ideas for modern Hellenic summer solstice festivals, but none of them really appealed to me. They all seemed a little too forced, and while I certainly have no problem with modern invention, they also seemed to claim ancient precedence where there was none as far as I could see. In that hymn, however, I found a piece of literary evidence giving a mythological explanation for the lengthening of days in the summer, and I thought it would be wonderful to create a festival around that concept. Since it was Artemis' dance that caused Helios to pause and watch, I also drew inspiration from one of the Homeric hymns to Artemis: She goes to Apollo's house to lead the dances of the Graces and Muses, and they all sing together.[127]

I swiftly discovered, however, that this alone would not make a good story. The divine dance already gave the festival a performing arts theme, so I wanted to present the myth of how the days became longer in some kind of skit or dramatization. In order to do that, however, I needed to add some element of conflict and resolution to make it an engaging tale. I was so pleased at having found an ancient account of the long days of summer that I didn't want to change that part of the story, so I decided to add to it instead. The ancient myth explains how the days get longer, but says nothing about what happens when the days get shorter. Consequently, I created a story about how the excessive heat of summer would cause crops to die, and so the people of Earth try to find a way to end the dance, but ultimately appeal to Zeus, Who restores order. This story, which I can only hope was divinely inspired, worked out beautifully well for our festival. It expresses the carefree joy of long summer days, but also reminds us that too much of anything can be detrimental.

The name Philokhoria is a word I created which would loosely translate to "loving the dance", a phrase that is exceptionally fitting for this festival. The official date of the Philokhoria would, of course, be the day of the summer solstice.

Celebrating the Philokhoria

To create your own Philokhoria celebration you will need one tea light or votive candle for each participant, a candle snuffer, a few pairs of scissors and enough paper or cardboard such that each participant can create their own model sun, some kind of music player and plenty of music, drums or any portable instruments or sound makers you can find, and whatever props or costumes you decide to use for your own rendition of the Philokhoria myth and any other performances you wish to put on.

When participants arrive, have each person cut out their own paper sun to be given to Helios as an offering. Each participant should also pick out a votive candle or tea light. Both of these items should either be carried along in the procession or set in the ritual space ahead of time.

The procession for the Philokhoria should be as dramatic and flamboyant as possible. If you can, have a pair of individuals, perhaps the acting priest and priestess, lead the procession dressed up and acting the parts of Artemis and Apollo. Mimesis, especially on the part of priests and priestesses, was fairly common in ancient Greece,[128] and it gives a lovely extra dramatic flair to a festival that celebrates the performing arts. Whoever you choose to lead the procession thus should be the same individuals who will be playing the parts of Artemis and Apollo in the dramatization of the Philokhoria myth.

When the barley prayer is complete, have the acting priest and priestess speak a prayer to Helios in celebration of the light of summer. Then have each participant come forward to the shrine or altar and light their votive candle or tea light, all together if you wish or, if you prefer, one at a time with their own individual prayers. With the shrine or altar thus filled with burning light, begin your presentation of the Philokhoria myth.

The story goes like this: Artemis was wandering the wilderness one day when She felt inclined to dance. She summoned the nearby nymphs and they began to sing and dance together. Apollo saw this and thought it was a wonderful idea, so He came with His lyre to add to the music, and summoned the Muses and Graces to join along. This performance was so magnificent that Helios stopped his chariot in the sky so that he could watch, causing the days to grow longer.

At first this was wonderful for Gods and mortals alike. Everyone had more time to be outdoors and enjoy summer's warmth, but as the dance grew longer, so did the days, and soon the Earth became so hot that crops began to die and people began to go hungry. Humans grew anxious, and thus decided to try to end the dance so that the days would grow shorter again. First the people chose the most beautiful young woman among them and set her on the horizon. "Look how that lovely woman gazes at the sun!" they shouted to one another. "Surely she must be in love with the God Helios!" But Helios would not turn his gaze to see the beautiful woman meant to lure Him down.

Next the people captured the most beautiful stag they could find and released it into the clearing where Artemis was dancing. "Look at the magnificent beast that runs there!" they shouted to one another. "What great hunter will bring down such a noble creature?" Missing only a single step in Her divine dance, Artemis picked up Her bow and shot the deer, having just barely stopped dancing when She began again. She did this so smoothly, it seemed the shot was a part of the dance itself.

Next the people chose the most beautiful young man[129] among them and sent him to distract Apollo from His music making. "Look at that handsome man!" they shouted to one another. "Surely he gazes at Apollo with love in his eyes!" Apollo turned to look at the young man, never lifting his nimble fingers from His lyre, and agreed that he was quite lovely. "You are fit to join our performance," He said to the young man. "Come, take up an instrument and make music with me." No wise mortal would decline such an invitation, so the young man joined Apollo's song.

Finally the people beseeched Zeus. "We shall all die if this dance continues so long, and the Gods will be left with no one to worship Them!" they cried. Zeus, knowing that order must be maintained, came down to the clearing where Artemis danced and firmly told the group to disperse. "Surely this has been a beauteous performance, but the seasons must progress and balance must be restored." Neither Apollo nor Artemis nor Helios, nor the nymphs, Graces nor Muses would argue with the King of the Gods, so they went along their way and would return to the dance another time when the seasons had run their course.

This myth can be presented in a myriad of ways. You might want to script your own version of the myth and present it as a play, or if you enjoy dramatic storytelling, you might just want to have someone act out each of the parts as a narrator reads the story. If you do decide to present the myth as a skit or play, it might be a good idea to cast someone as a narrator who can explain the plot to the audience, or you could write enough dialogue between the characters such that the plot will be easily understood. Your cast can be as large or as small as you choose. If your group has many people who want to participate in the reenactment, then you could cast the parts of Artemis, Apollo, Helios, Zeus, nine Muses, three Graces, the stag, the beautiful woman, the handsome man, and as many nymphs and humans as you like. If your group is particularly averse to putting on group performances, then perhaps a single storyteller acting out the myth on her own would be more your style.

Audience participation can be a wonderful way to get everyone involved and engaged in the myth. At our first presentation of the Philokhoria, our cast consisted of six people: Artemis, Apollo, Helios, Zeus, a nymph, and a narrator who also served as the voice of the people. When it came time for the humans to try to disrupt the dance, the narrator chose people from the audience to act as the stag, the beautiful woman, and the handsome man.

Your props can also be as simple or as complicated as you see fit. You might want to go all out with costumes, makeup, and stage lighting, or you might want to forego props altogether and let the acting designate who is playing which characters. A few simple props can be an excellent way to show who's who. Apollo can hold a small harp, lyre, or even a guitar (arguably the modern equivalent of the lyre), Artemis could wear a *khiton*[130] or a quiver (and probably ought to have a bow or toy bow nearby), Helios could wear or carry a symbol of the sun, Zeus could wear a crown or carry a lightning bolt, the stag could wear the type of deer antler headband so common around Christmas time, and the beautiful woman and handsome man could hold a rose in their teeth as they try to lure Helios and Apollo.

The Philokhoria myth can be enacted as seriously or comically as you desire. At our very first presentation of the myth, when the people had failed to distract Helios, Artemis, and Apollo, the narrator simply cried out "DAAAAAAAAD!" to call on Zeus as a child might call for their parent when a sibling isn't playing fair. In response, the man playing Zeus stepped out and shouted, "Kids! Time for bed!" As amusing as it sounds, it all fit perfectly well, and expressed both the jovial feel of the festival as a whole and the necessity for order and balance to be maintained.

When you have finished your presentation of the myth, gather all the participants around the altar or shrine where you lit your tea lights or votive candles. Have the acting priest and priestess say a prayer to Artemis, Helios, and Apollo. Thank Them for the long days of summer, and express your appreciation for light. Then instruct each participant to snuff out their tea light or votive candle and keep it. These candles can be a symbol for the warm light of the sun, a way to celebrate the summer dance even as it wanes, and a way to remember the heat of summer even in the dark of winter. As a gift in return for these candles, have each participant offer their paper sun to Helios, Artemis and Apollo. You might want to burn the suns in the altar fire, or place them as gifts on the altar or shrine, or let each participant decide what they feel would be the most fitting way to offer their model sun.

When everyone has finished trading suns for candles, gather the participants together again in a circle. Explain that in the ancient world the Greeks would hymn their Gods with elaborately crafted songs, but even without these beautiful pieces we can still raise our voices in celebration of Them. Encourage each person to sing a simple tone on whatever vowel they like in whatever range feels most comfortable. Tell them to listen to the sound, to feel the people around them as a community and to hear the chord they create as a hymn to the Gods.

Explain that after you have held this simple starting tone for a few minutes, people should feel free to change their note as they see fit, listening to the people around them and letting song and sensation determine what harmonies emerge. Let the music go as long as it will, swelling and changing until it slowly quiets to stillness.

With this activity everyone can participate in making music together, no matter how tone-deaf they think they are. You will find that the patterns of dissonance and resolution that arise will be beautiful regardless of what skill or talent your group does or does not have. Simply accept the song for what it is, and let it be a hymn to the summer dance.

When you've finished singing your wordless hymn, it's time for an activity I've come to call the "faster dance". First explain that the activity will consist of both dancing and music making, and let each person choose which of these roles they wish to participate in. Next gather all the dancers and teach them a simple dance step that can be danced in a circle. This could be a simple grapevine step or a complicated dance move you invented. Choose something that will work well for your group, and make sure everyone can easily perform it before you begin. Then have each of the music makers take up an instrument and begin playing music with a simple, slow, steady beat. Tell the dancers to begin their circle dance, at first moving slowly in time with the music. When everyone seems to have it down pretty well, instruct the music makers to slowly pick up the tempo, gradually playing faster to see if the dancers can keep up. Don't speed things up too quickly; let the dancers have a chance to adapt to see just how fast they can really go. Keep gradually increasing the speed, faster and faster until the dancers can no longer keep the steps. Despite the fact that my legs and feet are not particularly coordinated, every time I've participated in this activity it has been as a dancer. I've always enjoyed it, and it always ends with tons of good-natured laughter all around.

After the faster dance it's time to invite participants to give their own solo performances. This should be encouraged, but not required. If you like, you can let people know before hand that they will have an opportunity to perform their own song or dance, or you can just see what people feel inspired to present at the time. I love to spin fire poi, so I will include a poi performance in the Philokhoria whenever there is space to do it safely. You do not need to limit these performances to just singing, playing music, or dancing. If you like, you can let people give any sort of performance they wish to add to the Philokhoria.

When your performances are done, enjoy your Theoxenia feast. You might want to organize it as a barbeque or a picnic. Linger in the sunlight for as long as you can. If you like, include some outdoor sports or picnic games in the day's activities. Do whatever you like that helps you enjoy and embrace summer.

I should note here that despite the prominence of nymphs in the Philokhoria myth, I have not included any special ritual actions honoring them. There are two main reasons for this. First, Artemis was not normally worshipped along with the nymphs in ancient Greece.[131] They do appear with Her occasionally in myth, but their function in this regard seems to be rather limited.[132] Secondly, the nymphs themselves, as I understand them, are not a group of deities that are the same wherever you go. They are intimately connected with the particular features of the land. Every tree or spring or cave or stone will have its own nymph or nymphs. I feel that ritual actions meant to honor the nymphs ought to be tailored both to the specific nymph or group of nymphs, and to the natural feature she or they are associated with. If you feel that the nymphs present in your land ought to be honored at the Philokhoria, then by all means do so. Create a ritual that is specific to them and their features, and include it in your Philokhoria festival whenever you feel is most appropriate.[133]

The Philokhoria is both a celebration of summer's height and acceptance of its inevitable decline. We honor Apollo and Artemis for their beautiful summer song and dance, and we honor Helios for his golden warmth, but we know that these things can't continue unchanged eternally. The Philokhoria should help participants feel that they are enjoying and living their summer, that even though it must eventually end, they are still getting the most out of it. Hopefully people can also carry this lesson on to the rest of their lives. By living each moment of our lives to its fullest, with joy and celebration despite its sorrows and losses, we can be sure that we have lived our lives well and fully without wasting a single minute. Every summer must end, but they can end with the satisfaction of time well spent, and with anticipation of summers to come.

Artemis and Apollo. (Archaeological Museum of Delphi)

Conclusion

How To Do It Alone

The Cataleos festivals were designed to be group celebrations, but not everyone has people to worship with. Some prefer a solitary path, whereas others simply don't know of anyone nearby who would want to join them. I encourage people of the latter group to explore their local community, discreetly if need be, and discover if there might be any like-minded folk nearby after all. You never know who might be interested in the idea once they hear about it. While I vehemently disagree with proselytizing, I see nothing wrong with advertising.

Even so, sometimes you must worship alone, and some people prefer a solitary religion. I encourage readers not to miss celebrating the Cataleos festivals solely because they have no one to worship with. If you have no one to celebrate with, be it by choice or by circumstance, here are some ideas for how to adapt the Cataleos festivals to solitary practice.

When you prepare for your festival, have everything you will need ready and waiting in the ritual space. Choose one item, ideally one that is symbolic of the festival you are celebrating, and choose this one to carry in your procession. Any of the festival activities I described can be performed alone. If you find a situation where two things are usually done at once, simply do them both yourself sequentially, or pick whichever one you feel is most important and do that one. For the various competitions, find some way to test yourself. The purpose of the *agon* is not to prove who is best, but to motivate everyone to improve themselves. If the contest was a relay race, then perhaps see how far you can run before you tire, or run a race twice and see if you can beat your first time on the second try. If the contest was archery, then perhaps shoot six rounds and see if each time you can beat your previous score. Even a Theoxenia feast can be celebrated alone. Simply cook or buy yourself a splendid dinner, give a portion from each part of it to Artemis, and invite Her to dine with you. You might find that some exceptionally interesting thoughts pop into your mind as you eat.

Cleaning Up

At the end of a festival you will find that there is more to cleaning up than just putting away your ritual items. You will have a variety of libations and offerings that ought to be attended to properly. There is no single acceptable way of dealing with these items. As with everything else, each group or temple has its own preferences and customs.

Libations and food offerings will be your most immediate concern. I know of two particularly popular methods of disposal. One is to leave out the offerings for a while, and then, just before they begin to look unappealing, pour the libations down a drain and throw away the food. The idea behind this practice is that while the food and drink are left out for the Gods, They will take from it whatever essence They can get out of it, and then you dispose of what is left. However, for some (especially those who celebrate their festivals indoors) leaving out food and drink can attract insects or other unwelcome pests, making this disposal method somewhat impractical.

I prefer the other popular method of dealing with food and drink offerings. Directly after a festival, I take the libations and food offerings to some convenient and relatively secluded place outdoors and leave them there for whatever creatures Artemis sends to receive them. If you choose to dispose of your libations and food offerings in this way, be sure that the food and drink you leave will not be harmful to the environment. Organic foods are much less likely to harm local wildlife than processed foods filled with artificial additives. If you are particularly concerned about animals coming by to eat what you leave out, you could always dig a small hole and bury the offerings. While this was typically done for khthonic deities rather than Olympians such as Artemis, I'm sure that She will appreciate the intent to protect your local wildlife.

At the end of a festival you will probably also be left with some other, non-edible offerings. You have a number of options for these items. If you have a temple or sacred space devoted to Artemis or to all the Gods, you might choose to leave the offerings there. In this case, I would recommend you put them on display somewhere, even if only for a while. If you hold festivals regularly, you will eventually find that you have more offerings than you have space for. In this case, you might want to go out and bury some of the offerings, perhaps in a special box decorated for Artemis, keeping only the most exceptional pieces to adorn the temple.[134] Alternatively, you might find that you can put the offerings to use somehow. If you do decide to utilize them, be sure that whatever purpose they are put to will ultimately honor Artemis, as they were intended for Her.

If you don't have a sacred space that is always set aside for worship, then you might encourage each of the participants to take their offerings home with them and do with them as they see fit. If they have a personal shrine to Artemis or to all the Gods, encourage them to set their offerings on their shrine for Her. If they don't, then perhaps they should find some personal location where they can leave the offering for Her. Alternatively, if people leave their offerings with you and you have no shrine or sacred space in which to place them for Artemis, then you might find some spot in the wilderness or an especially pretty tree or stone in your local park and leave the offerings for Her there. You never know who might be unexpectedly inspired when they happen to see them. Again, if you are concerned about local animals or wildlife being harmed by the offerings you leave, then you might consider burying them. Be sure that any offerings you leave outdoors are made of materials that will not be harmful to the environment. For example, some dyes or glues might pollute soil or rainwater. If you are concerned about this, consider leaving or burying the items in a sealed, decorative box. You could also make sure that the offerings are made from biodegradable materials in the first place, or just choose a different method of disposal. Again, if you decide to put the offerings to use somehow, make sure that they ultimately benefit Artemis in whatever purpose they serve.

Epilogue

The Cataleos festivals are meant to grow over time. I will most likely continue to add to them as I learn more about other ancient festivals, or as need or inspiration spur invention. Feel free to be creative with your own festivals. You most certainly can celebrate the Cataleos calendar as I have described it here, but if you want to use these ideas as a basis for creating your own festivals, then don't be afraid to invent your own calendar that specifically suits the needs of you and your people. I ask only that you be honest and clear about whatever you decide to do. If you celebrate Cataleos festivals, then say so. If you make up your own festivals, be proud of that, and tell people what you invented and why. If you recreate ancient festivals or include ancient ritual elements, explain where they come from and why you decided to use them.

Remember that the Cataleos festivals were originally designed to be public. They generally include activities that should be appropriate for any random group of people that decides to show up at a festival, or they are easily adaptable to any kind of group. The Cataleos festivals may not have the communal intensity of rituals designed for a closed working group whose members are intimately close to one another, but there still exists the potential for each person to have incredibly intense moments of communion with Artemis. Many of the most intense experiences you and your participants will have at Cataleos festivals will probably be private or internal. People will have stunning moments of personal revelation, or some activity will speak to them deeply. Participants who go just for the sake of going might not get much out of it, but people who sincerely put themselves into the festival are likely to achieve spectacular results.

Don't just follow this book blindly; experiment with your own rituals and find what speaks to you and your group. If you decide you like the Cataleos rituals as I have presented them, then explore them thoroughly. Find nuances of meaning that your group can share or discuss. Let your religion be personalized and personable.

There is, of course, more that could be said about each of the festivals I have mentioned, but I cannot possibly write it all. Some of the things you will learn about Artemis and about yourself at these celebrations can only be discovered through participation. Reading alone cannot provide what experience does. I encourage everyone to get up, get out, and encounter Artemis in your own wild, moonlit dance.

End Notes

---

[1] The word Hellenistai is a matter of some debate. I have heard that in academic circles related to Bible studies the word signifies a Greek Jew, but I have been unable to locate that exact word in any ancient Greek texts. In an email dialogue in July of 2006 on the mailing list *Neokoroi*, members discussed a number of possible words that could be used to describe our religion or its practitioners. Our intent was to establish a higher degree of clarity, not to sanction official terminology, as there is no group or organization within Hellenismos that could do such a thing. Of those terms raised in the discussion on *Neokoroi*, I like Hellenismos best to describe our religion, as there is at least some ancient precedence for it, and I like Hellenistai best to describe its practitioners, as it makes the most sense grammatically. Hellenistai would be the feminine plural form of the word, with Hellenistoi as the masculine plural, Helleniste as the feminine singular, and Hellenistos as the masculine singular, but I usually just use Hellenistai and Helleniste. There are many other terms commonly used to describe reconstructed ancient Greek religion and its practitioners, and many reasons to like or dislike each of those terms, but I must consider that debate beyond the scope of this book.

[2] Simon, Festivals of Attica: An Archaeological Commentary, 3.

[3] Simon, Festivals of Attica: An Archaeological Commentary, 4; there were exceptions to this: leap years included an extra month, and there were approximately three of these every eight years. The four year Olympiad, which came later, was a halving of this eight year cycle.

[4] Parke, Festivals of the Athenians, 81.

[5] Parke, Festivals of the Athenians, 55, 81, 97, 137, 146; Simon, Festivals of Attica: An Archaeological Commentary, 81; also see chapter 7.

[6] See chapter 2.

[7] Parke, Festivals of the Athenians, 18-25.

[8] Burkert, Greek Religion, 105-7. Homer's *Odyssey* also provides ample description of how any and every kind of sport would be part of a Hellenic festival. If your group is particularly fond of sports or contests, then feel free to include any variety of them in any of your celebrations.

[9] Burkert, Greek Religion, 75-9.

[10] While certainly unusual, priests of Artemis did exist. The only evidence of this I know of comes from Ephesos, where Artemis was served by eunuch priests (Xenophon, *Anabasis*, 5.3.6). In Virgil's *Aeneid*, after Hippolytus dies, Diana convinces Aesculapius to revive him (or uses Aesculapius's medicine to do so Herself, depending on the translation), renames him Virbius, then takes him to a secluded grove to hide him from Jupiter; from this a tradition is established where an escaped slave could become a priest of Diana (4.43). This is, however, a peculiarly Roman source, and has no Greek

equivalent. Thus it could arguably be said to illustrate some of the distinctive differences between Artemis and Diana, Who I believe to be separate entities.

[11] This passage has origins in two Greek phrases commonly used (or misused) in some modern Hellenic groups. These phrases are the source of constant controversy in Hellenismos. The first phrase *"Hekas, hekas o este bebeloi"* can be found in *Old Stones, New Temples*, by Drew Campbell. Its origin is extremely ambiguous; I have heard claims that it was used in the mysteries of Eleusis but have been unable to verify this. Even so, there is no ancient evidence or precedence for the use of this phrase in common festivals or everyday rituals. The second phrase, *"O theoi genoisthe apotropoi kakon"* can be found in a ritual called *A Group Offertory Rite in Greek and English* by Drew Campbell, which is posted at:

http://www.hellenion.org/campbella/group_drewcambell.html

While Campbell does cite a source for this phrase (Eur. Phoen. 586f., quoted in Pulleyn, p 64), I have been unable to verify it myself, and remain skeptical of its accuracy, since, as far as I know, the grammar of the phrase itself is incorrect. Furthermore, many modern Hellenistai have commented on how illogical and counterintuitive it is to call on the Gods to repel evil when They are never supposed to be in the presence of evil to begin with. All that said, I have found that including some simple Greek phrases in modern Hellenic ritual can be quite effective. The phrase I have devised – "*hekas, hekas, apotrepete kakon*" – would basically translate to "far away, far away, turn away evil". Exactly who is turning away evil is left purposefully ambiguous; you could direct the command to the spirits around you, perhaps the spirits of the land, hoping they will help turn away evil, or perhaps you will address the command to each other. Evil in this context is not evil in a Christian sense, but rather anything that is bad for ritual, unfit for the presence of the gods, impure, profane, etc. I have found that this phrase can help to purify an area that is not generally set aside for ritual (volumes could be said about the power of words alone, but I will not write about it here), and it can also call the attention of the participants and set the mood for a Hellenic ritual.

[12] Burkert, Greek Religion, 107.

[13] Burkert, Greek Religion, 107.

[14] Homer, *Odyssey*, 3.330-40.

[15] Simon, Festivals of Attica: An Archaeological Commentary, 83.

[16] Simon, Festivals of Attica: An Archaeological Commentary, 83; Cole, Landscapes, Gender, and Ritual Space: The Ancient Greek Experience, 227.

[17] Cole, Landscapes, Gender, and Ritual Space: The Ancient Greek Experience, 195.

[18] Cole, Landscapes, Gender, and Ritual Space: The Ancient Greek Experience, 195.

[19] Cole, Landscapes, Gender, and Ritual Space: The Ancient Greek Experience, 227.

[20] Simon, Festivals of Attica: An Archaeological Commentary, 86.

---

[21] For further discussion see Cole, Landscapes, Gender, and Ritual Space: The Ancient Greek Experience, 226-8; Simon, Festivals of Attica: An Archaeological Commentary, 83-8.

[22] Parke, Festivals of the Athenians, 139.

[23] Aristophanes, Lysistrata, 641-7.

[24] Vernant, Mortals and Immortals: Collected Essays, 217-8.

[25] Vernant, Mortals and Immortals: Collected Essays, 200, 217-9.

[26] Cole, Landscapes, Gender, and Ritual Space: The Ancient Greek Experience, 210-1.

[27] Evidence for this is ubiquitous. For further discussion see Simon, Festivals of Attica: An Archaeological Commentary, 85-86; Burkert, Greek Religion, 151; Vernant, Mortals and Immortals: Collected Essays, 200, 217-9; Connelly, Portrait of a Priestess: Women and Ritual in Ancient Greece, 32-3.

[28] Simon, Festivals of Attica: An Archaeological Commentary, 87-88.

[29] Simon, Festivals of Attica: An Archaeological Commentary, 83.

[30] Simon, Festivals of Attica: An Archaeological Commentary, 86.

[31] Simon, Festivals of Attica: An Archaeological Commentary, 83.

[32] References to the service of young girls at the cult of Artemis Brauronia are ubiquitous (Connelly, Portrait of a Priestess: Women and Ritual in Ancient Greece, 32-3; Vernant, Mortals and Immortals: Collected Essays, 200; etc.). A particularly famous passage from Aristophanes' Lysistrata (641-7) mentions serving as an *arktos* among other ritual activities. While many scholars believe these other activities to be in the service of different deities, in his article "Artemis Bear-Leader" (The Classical Quarterly, New Series, Vol. 31, No. 2. 1981, pp. 276-281.), Mark B. Walbank brings to light compelling evidence that each of these activities were performed in honor of Artemis Brauronia by girls at a specific age.

[33] Vernant, Mortals and Immortals: Collected Essays, 198.

[34] Simon, Festivals of Attica: An Archaeological Commentary, 87; Burkert Greek Religion, 70.

[35] While Hekate most definitely has an identity of Her own in the modern day, Rudloff eloquently articulates the problems with establishing an independent identity for Her in the ancient world (Hekate in Ancient Greek Religion, 62-3). In ancient Attica (the district in which Athens, Brauron and Eleusis were all located) Hekate was generally equated with Artemis from the fifth century B.C.E. onwards (Burkert, Greek Religion, 171; Euripides, *Phoenissae*, 109-110), and Artemis was sometimes addressed as Artemis Hekate (Aeschylus, *Suppliant Women*, 667; see also). Rudloff thoroughly explores the various ways in which these two goddesses both converged and diverged in Hekate in Ancient Greek Religion. I feel that I can say with certainty, however, that "Hekate" is both an epithet and aspect of Artemis as well as a separate Goddess in Her own right.

[36] Brauron no. 1271

[37] Spawforth, The Complete Greek Temples, 79-80; wreathes were another popular form of statue adornment, and there were many more less common methods of icon adoration.

[38] Minai, *The Virgin Goddess*, He Epistole, Spring 2006, 10. Most of my research for this essay came from Greek Virginity by Giulia Sissa.

[39] Burkert, Greek Religion, 130.

[40] However much modern Neo-Pagans would like to believe that Artemis partook in lesbianism, there is simply no ancient evidence to support it.

[41] Burkert, Greek Religion, 130.

[42] Even priestesses were expected to marry eventually. Virginity was almost never a lifelong requirement, but rather a requirement of certain positions that would be held only temporarily. For more information, see Connelly, Portrait of a Priestess: Women and Ritual in Ancient Greece, 41.

[43] These various versions and many more can be found in multiple sources. Each of the versions I have presented can be found in *The Library of Greek Mythology* by Apollodoros (8.2), *The Constellations* by Eratosthenes or Pseudo-Eratosthenes (1), or *Poetic Astronomy* by Hyginus (2.1).

[44] Parke, Festivals of the Athenians, 138; Simon, Festivals of Attica: An Archaeological Commentary, 81.

[45] Parke, Festivals of the Athenians, 137.

[46] Parke, Festivals of the Athenians, 138.

[47] Parke, Festivals of the Athenians, 138.

[48] Parke, Festivals of the Athenians, 138. Parke also notes the similarity between this myth and the foundation myth of Brauron.

[49] Vernant, Mortals and Immortals: Collected Essays, 215-6.

[50] Simon, Festivals of Attica: An Archaeological Commentary, 81; Parke, Festivals of the Athenians, 138.

[51] Cited by Parke in Festivals of the Athenians, 138.

[52] Parke, Festivals of the Athenians, 138; he also concludes that the *amphiphontes* were offered to "Artemis as a moon goddess" on p. 189.

[53] Simon, Festivals of Attica: An Archaeological Commentary, 81.

[54] Vernant, Mortals and Immortals: Collected Essays, 248.

[55] Simon, Festivals of Attica: An Archaeological Commentary, 81-2.

[56] Callimachus, Hymn III, 38-9. This may have been an extension of Her liminal aspect, which both Cole (Landscapes, Gender, and Ritual Space: The Ancient Greek Experience) and Vernant (Mortals and Immortals: Collected Essays) discuss repeatedly.

[57] Parke, Festivals of the Athenians, 137; Simon, Festivals of Attica: An Archaeological Commentary, 79-81.

[58] Parke, Festivals of the Athenians, 137.

[59] Burkert, Greek Religion, 151.

[60] Cole, Landscapes, Gender, and Ritual Space: The Ancient Greek Experience, 206-7.

[61] Parke, Festivals of the Athenians, 149-50.

[62] Parke, Festivals of the Athenians, 150-1.

[63] The preliminary sacrifices for battle described by Vernant in Mortals and Immortals: Collected Essays show obvious participation of men in Artemisian worship, and the Athenian *Kharisteria, Elaphebolia, Mounukhia* and *Thargelia* festivals certainly would have had male participation. Xenophon describes how men in Sparta would have dedicated garlands to Artemis upon returning from a gymnasium (Minor Works, Agesilaus 1.27), and Euripides's *Hippolytos* could also serve as evidence that men worshipped Artemis as well as women.

[64] Hippolytos would be the typical example of this. See Euripides, *Hippolytos*, especially line 1398.

[65] Euripides, *Hippolytos*, 1330-1334.

[66] Oinokhoe in a Neokoroi discussion, July 21, 2007.

[67] Many modern Neo-Pagans argue that Artemis' silver bow is clearly analogous to the Moon, but actually Her bow was made from a variety of different materials that changed depending on the author and the specific source. According to Callimachus, Apollo's bow is made of gold (Hymn II) and Artemis's of silver (Hymn III), although Her arms, belt, chariot, and the bridles with which she yoked deer to her chariot were all golden (Hymn III). In the Homeric Hymns, Apollo's bow is silver (Hymn III, IX) but His sword is golden (Hymn XXVII), and Artemis's bow is golden (Hymn XXVII). Mythology is full of instances where various Gods had items made from gold, and we cannot assume that each one of these is somehow connected with the sun. Rather they are meant to symbolize that all possessions of the Gods are immensely valuable, incredibly beautiful, and crafted from the best materials. Furthermore, it seems Artemis and Apollo could each have either the silver or the gold bow, as long as the other had the opposite metal. Thus it is far more likely that the bows of Artemis and Apollo were made of gold and silver so that the Twins could have weapons made from twin precious metals; it emphasized Their relationship to each other rather than symbolizing any supposed relationship to the Sun or Moon.

[68] I personally find it highly unlikely. I have yet to see any convincing evidence of actual human sacrifice for Artemis, only mythological accounts that are probably more allegorical than historical. That said, some scholars may disagree with me, although I find their supporting evidence to be tenuous at best.

[69] Cole, Landscapes, Gender, and Ritual Space: The Ancient Greek Experience, 18-9.

[70] Rule, *Artemis*, Deity.

[71] Otto, The Homeric Gods, 84; Aeschylus, *Agamemnon*, 135-45.

[72] Cunningham, Cunningham's Encyclopedia of Magical Herbs, 227.

[73] Pindar, Pythian Ode 2.11.

[74] Simon, Festivals of Attica: An Archaeological Commentary, 82.

[75] Simon, Festivals of Attica: An Archaeological Commentary, 82; Parke, Festivals of Attica: An Archaeological Commentary, 54-5.

[76] Vernant, Mortals and Immortals: Collected Essays, 247.

[77] Simon (Festivals of Attica: An Archaeological Commentary, 82) points out that, according to Aristotle, this sacrifice was promised to Enyalios as well.

[78] Parke, Festivals of the Athenians, 55; Simon, Festivals of Attica: An Archaeological Commentary, 82.

[79] Parke (Festivals of the Athenians, 56) notes that the sixth of *Boedromion* had already been established as a festival for Artemis Agrotera.

[80] Parke, Festivals of the Athenians, 55; Simon, Festivals of Attica: An Archaeological Commentary, 82.

[81] Simon, Festivals of Attica: An Archaeological Commentary, 82; Parke, Festivals of the Athenians, 55.

[82] Parke, Festivals of the Athenians, 55.

[83] Artemis would receive a preliminary sacrifice before battle, and would also intervene when a people were facing a conflict where the only possible results were victory or complete annihilation. For full discussion see Vernant, Mortals and Immortals: Collected Essays, 203, 244-57.

[84] Vernant, Mortals and Immortals: Collected Essays, "Artemis and Preliminary Sacrifice in Combat," 244-57.

[85] Parke, Festivals of the Atheniana, 55.

[86] Vernant, Mortals and Immortals: Collected Essays, 291; Burkert, Greek Religion, 55; Connelly, Portrait of a Priestess: Women and Ritual in Ancient Greece, 179; Parke, Festivals of the Athenians, 18-21; etc.

[87] Vernant, Mortals and Immortals: Collected Essays, 290-302; Burkert, Greek Religion, 55-59; Connelly, Portrait of a Priestess: Women and Ritual in Ancient Greece, 179; Parke, Festivals of the Athenians, 18-21; etc.

[88] Burkert, Greek Religion, 57.

[89] This passage is effectively a summary of what Burkert wrote on pages 55-59 of Greek Religion There he gives a clear, concise, and detailed description of *thusia*, and discusses the meaning behind some of the finer points.

[90] Homer, *Odyssey*, 3.330-40.

[91] Parke, Festivals of the Athenians, 19.

---

[92] One example of the ideal victim can be found in the *Odyssey*, where Nestor promises to sacrifice to Athena a cow that has never been put to work (Homer, *Odyssey*, 3.380).

[93] I shall spare the reader my usual rant about PETA and instead encourage everyone to take a closer look at the organization and discover for themselves what skeletons lie in the closet.

[94] Burkert, Greek Religion, 152.

[95] Animal-shaped cakes were used as substitutes for real animals in the *Elaphebolia* and the *Diasia*. See Pakre, Festivals of the Athenians for further discussion.

[96] Raven Kaldera, private email, August 6, 2007. For further discussion of animal sacrifice in modern Neo-Paganism, see *Towards A Better Understanding: Animal Sacrifice And The Community*, by Raven Kaldera at:
http://www.cauldronfarm.com/asphodel/articles/towards_a_better_understanding.html

[97] While there are various accounts of human sacrifice in ancient sources, these are almost always associated with some foreign, barbaric people, and are frequently mythological. It is unlikely that the ancient Greeks ever actually performed human sacrifice themselves.

[98] Euripides, *Iphigenia Among the Taurians*, 1462-5.

[99] Euripides, *Iphigenia Among the Taurians*, 1460.

[100] Simon, Festivals of Attica: An Archaeological Commentary, 81; Parke, Festivals of the Athenians, 125.

[101] Parke, Festivals of the Athenians, 125.

[102] Simon, Festivals of Attica: An Archaeological Commentary, 81; Parke, Festivals of the Athenians, 125.

[103] Parke, Festivals of the Athenians, 125.

[104] Xenophon, *On Hunting*, I.17-8.

[105] Xenophon, *On Hunting*, II.1

[106] There are admittedly many styles of modern bow available today that are not so primitive. Compound bows allow people to pull a much heavier draw than they would otherwise be capable of, and while they make fine weapons, they still feel like cheating to me. Recurve bows can come with a wide variety of attachments and enhancements that are invaluable for target competitions, but for hunting I prefer a simple, unadorned recurve. I've also seen longbows and shortbows with a similar graceful simplicity.

[107] Hunting seasons vary by state (and sometimes even by county) and are restricted by the species of prey and the weapon used. For more information, contact your state's wildlife organization.

[108] Apollodorus, *The Library*, 3.30.

---

[109] The interdependence of predator and prey is even further illustrated by the fact that Artemis Herself can transform into a deer (Apollodorus, *The Library*, 1.7.4). She is not only the Huntress but the hunted as well.

[110] Chrimes, Anicent Sparta: A Re-Examination of the Evidence, 251.

[111] Chrimes, Anicent Sparta: A Re-Examination of the Evidence, 124; Vernant, Mortals and Immortals: Collected Essays, 227.

[112] Vernant, Mortals and Immortals: Collected Essays, 226.

[113] Vernant, Mortals and Immortals: Collected Essays, 243. Burkert (Greek Religion, 151) claims it was the Spartan girls who wore these masks, but Verenant's essays are considerably more recent. In this case Burkert's research may be outdated by comparison.

[114] Homeric Hymn 9. Furthermore, model horses were found in the sanctuary of Artemis Orthia at Sparta, and can be seen today on display in the museum there. Artemis was also said to have helped Hieron master his horses and thus win a chariot race (Pindar, Pythian 2.8).

[115] This image is clearly identified as Artemis by Pausanias (*Description of Greece*, 5.19.5). Chrimes also uses the image of Potnia Theron to establish the identity of Artemis Orthia in Sparta (Ancient Sparta: A Re-examination of the Evidence, 248-51).

[116] Parke, Festivals of the Athenians, 146.

[117] Chrimes, Ancient Sparts: A Re-Examination of the Evidence, 260; Parke, Festivals of the Athenians, 146.

[118] Parke, Festivals of the Athenians, 146.

[119] Parke, Festivals of the Athenians, 146.

[120] Parke, Festivals of the Athenians, 146-7; Simon, Festivals of Attica: An Archaeological Commentary, 77-8.

[121] Parke, Festivals of the Athenians, 147-8; Simon, Festivals of Attica: An Archaeological Commentary, 78.

[122] Chrimes, Ancient Sparta: A Re-Examination of the Evidence, 260-272.

[123] Parke, Festivals of the Athenians, 146.

[124] Zaidman and Pantel, Religion in the Ancient Greek City, 47.

[125] Homeric Hymn III; Callimachus, Hymn IV; etc.

[126] Callimachus, Hymn III, 170-82, trans. A. W. Mair and G. R. Mair.

[127] Homeric Hymn XXVII, 11-20, trans. Evelyn-White.

[128] Connelly, Portrait of a Priestess: Women and Ritual in Ancient Greece, 104-15.

[129] This myth was originally designed to embrace both heterosexuality and homosexuality. If your group is uncomfortable with homosexual themes, then another equally valid version of the myth would have a young woman sent to distract Apollo, whom Apollo then recruits to join Artemis's dance.

---

[130] See appendix 2.

[131] Larson, Greek Nymphs: Myth, Cult, Lore, 108.

[132] The nymphs generally seem to appear either as dancing partners of Artemis, particularly as mythic symbols of adolescent girls, or as Her handmaidens. Personally, I have always found the connection evocative of a fairy queen among fairies. In Greek Nymphs: Myth, Cult Lore, Larson thoroughly explains what connection the nymphs might have had with Artemis in ancient Greece, and what role they played with Her. See especially pages 107-10.

[133] Greek Nymphs: Myth, Cult, Lore by Larson can provide plenty of inspiration on how to effectively accomplish this.

[134] In popular ancient Greek temples, the less valuable offerings would be periodically buried, while the more expensive offerings would become carefully kept temple assets (Burkert, Greek Religion, 94).

Appendices

Appendix 1: A List of Dates

Cataleos Festivals:

March 6 .... Arkteia
Full Moon in April .... Mounukhia
May 6-7 .... Thargelia
June 6 .... Artemisia
Summer Solstice .... Philokhoria
September 6 .... Kharisteria
October 6 .... Elaphebolia
December 6 .... Theronia

Appendix 2: How to Make a Peplos and a Khiton

To make a simple peplos or khiton you will need a large piece of cloth, a rope or something to use as a belt, and some pins or buttons. The length of the cloth will determine how long the garment is. Usually I measure from my shoulders to my knees, but some people enjoy the look of longer garments, in which case you could measure as far down as your ankles. The width of the garment should be twice the distance between your forearms. For a chiton, you might want to make the cloth even wider, allowing for more dramatic folds on the sleeves. For a peplos, you might want to make the cloth a little narrower, allowing for a closer-fitting, less bulky garment. As a general rule, the larger your piece of cloth is, the more folds you will be able to get, and the more bulky the end result will be. (Fig. 1 & 2)

Once you have your piece of cloth ready, fold it in half so that the width is once again the distance you measured. For a modest look you could sew the ends together, resulting in a wide tube of cloth, or you could just leave the garment open along one side. (Fig. 3)

Next at the center of your folded cloth, pin the garment at about where your shoulders will be. (Fig. 4) To prevent the garment from constantly falling off your shoulders, you might want to move the pins in towards each other a bit on the back fold and away from each other on the front fold. This way the back of the garment will hold the shoulders together and the front will have a nicely scooped neck line.

If you're making a peplos, all you have to do now is put the garment on so that your head goes between the shoulder pins, and your arms go through what was the top of the tube of cloth. Then tie a cord or belt around your waist. (Fig. 5)

If you're making a khiton, continue placing pins along the top of the garment at even intervals. (Fig. 6) Your head goes through the two pins at the center, and the space between the last pin and the edge of the cloth on either side is where your arms go through, making a sort of elegantly draped sleeve. Finish it of by tying a cord or belt around your waist. (Fig. 7)

If you don't have any decorative pins to use at the top of the garment, you could instead find some nice looking buttons and sew them to the garment at the same place you would have put the pins. If you choose to go this route, you will probably want to pin the garment with safety pins first and try it on to make sure that everything sits in the right place.

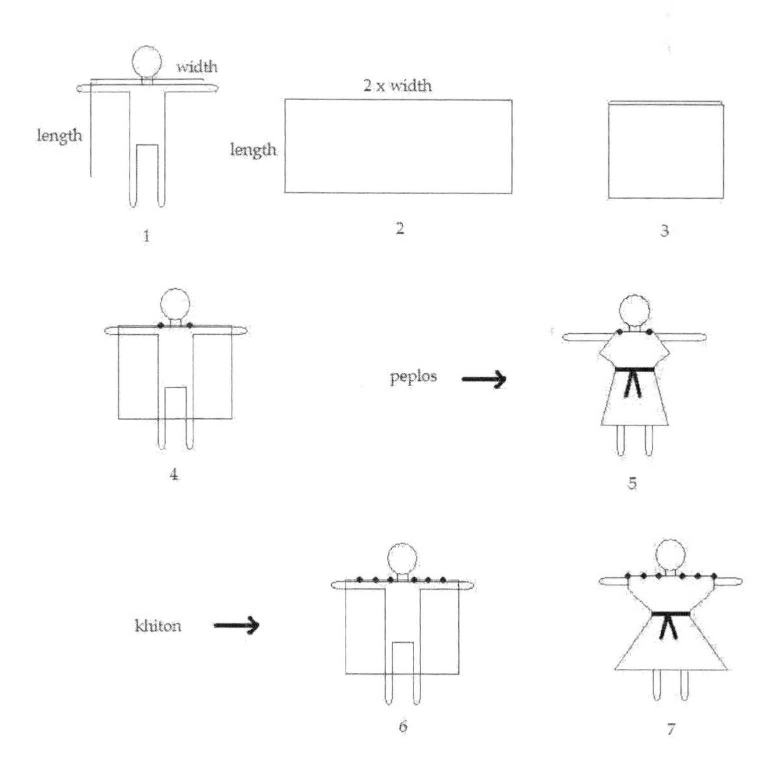

Appendix 3: The Artemis Oracle

The Artemis Oracle is a divination tool I created specifically to aid communication with Artemis. There was no ancient Greek oracle or divinatory method specific to Artemis that I know of; this is a completely modern invention. I decided to create an Artemisian oracle because I wanted a method of divination that I could use to communicate with by Artemis myself. I began studying Tarot when I was thirteen, and even though I can read well enough for other people, I have extreme difficulty doing my own readings. The strength of the Artemis Oracle seems to be in its ability to allow one to read for oneself. When I bring it out at festivals, I lend my aid in interpretation when people request it, but that occurs rarely, and I encourage people to interpret the results on their own.

The Artemis Oracle is designed to combine various words in multiples of six that will create phrases that the reader can interpret. It consists of 144 vocabulary words, six pairs of words that make polar opposites, and twenty context words, prefixes, or suffixes, each repeated three times, to create a grand total of 216 words – 6^3.

To create your own Artemis Oracle, you will need to find 216 small sticks or stones that you can mark or carve the various words onto. They should all be about the same size, and you will need to make or buy some kind of bag or box that you can put them all into.

To use the Artemis Oracle, simply draw a number of sticks or stones out of your bag or box, one at a time without looking at them, and set them in front of you in the order that you drew them. For a very simple question, you might just need to pull out a single word. For a more complex question you could draw six, and for particularly complicated issues you could set out six stanzas of six words each. For the Mounukhia, I usually have participants draw six words.

Interpretation is extremely personal. The phrases you get will rarely form coherent sentences, but will usually instead mimic the nearly incoherent prophesies of an oracle gone mad with divine presence. The words themselves will mean different things to different people, and the way they combine might jump out to someone as being particularly symbolic of something going on in their life, or they might remain a mystery until something happens to shed light on the reading.

If you were planning to only draw one word and the one you pull out is a context word, that usually means that either She doesn't want to answer your question, or you need to draw five more words. Your own intuition can tell you which is the case.

These are the 216 words that make up the Artemis Oracle:

Pair Words:
Darkness/Light
Day/Night
Fear/Courage
Life/Death
Pain/Pleasure
Predator/Prey

Vocabulary Words:
Achieve
Aim
Animal
Archery
Arrow
Bear
Beast
Bestial
Birth
Black
Blue
Boar
Boundary
Bow
Bright
Brother
Brown
Burn
Cat
Chase
Child
Chorus
Cliff
Complete
Compound
Bow
Confidence
Courageous
Creature
Crown
Cruel
Cub
Dance
Dark
Daughter
Dawn
Decide
Decision
Deer
Defend
Discern
Doe
Dog
Draw
Earth
Father
Faun
Ferocious
Fire
Fly
Forest
Free
Freedom
Frightened
Garland
Gentle
Give Birth
Golden
Green
Grotto
Harbor
Harmony
Harsh
Hawk
Horse
Hound

Hunt
Hunter
Illuminate
Immortal
Independence
Instinct
Intuition
Javelin
Kill
Lake
Learn
Liberate
Light
Lion
Lithe
Meadow
Moon
Moonrise
Moonset
Mother
Mountain
Move
Music
Nature
Nymph
Ocean
Prepare
Pride
Proud
Pure
Raise
Recurve Bow
Red
Release
Ride
River
Road
Run
Runner
Sacrifice
Shady
Shaft
Sharp
Shoot
Sibling
Silver
Sing
Sister
Slaughter
Slay
Snake
Son
Song
Speak
Stag
Star
Strong
Sun
Sunrise
Sunset
Survive
Swim
Tender
Torch
Tough
Travel
Tree
Twilight
Twin
Virgin
Wait
Water
White
Wild
Wind
Wooded
Woods
Yellow
Young

Context Words:
and
because
but
for
from
future
in
-ing
-ly
my
nor
of
or
past
-s
that
to
un-
with
your

Annotated Bibliography of Secondary Sources

This is not meant to be a comprehensive list of all secondary sources useful to the study of Hellenismos. Instead it lists only the secondary sources I used in writing this book, as well as a few other texts I thought readers might find useful.

Blundell, Sue. Women in Ancient Greece. 1995. Cambridge, Massachusetts: Harvard University Press, 2001.

A fabulous book about women in ancient Greece. Chapter 3 contains some especially valuable insight regarding the nature of Artemis.

Boardman, John. The Greeks Overseas: Their Early Colonies and Trade. 4th ed. London: Thames and Hudson, 1999.

A decent textbook with some scattered information about Artemis as She was known in Greek colonies.

Burkert, Walter. Greek Religion. Trans. John Raffan. 1985. Cambridge, Massachusetts: Harvard University Press, 2000.

This is, in my opinion, the one book that every Helleniste should own. Despite the fact that some of the information is now out of date, this is still the most comprehensive book you can find on ancient Greek religion. The information is presented concisely and clearly and is easily accessible for anyone wanting to take a reconstructionist approach to their religion.

Burkert, Walter. Homo Necans: The Anthropology of Ancient Greek Sacrificial Ritual and Myth. Trans. Peter Bing. Berkeley, Los Angeles, London: University of California Press, 1983.

Burkert, Walter. Structure and History in Greek Mythology and Ritual. 1979. Berkeley, Los Angeles, London: University of California Press, 1982.

Interesting books that presents some fascinating information. Personally, I don't agree with all of Burkert's conclusions in this text. Some of them seem to stretch a bit too much. Even so, it's worth reading for the evidence it brings to light.

Campbell, Drew. Old Stones, New Temples: Ancient Greek Paganism Reborn. Xlibris Corporation, 2000.

Much to my dismay, this has become the most well known book on modern Hellenismos. I dislike it intensely, but it's worth referencing here because of its unfortunate popularity. When it was published, it was the only book out there about modern Hellenismos, but now there are much better texts available.

Cartledge, Paul. The Spartans: The World of the Warrior-Heroes of Ancient Greece. Woodstock & New York: The Overlook Press, 2003.

An excellent book about ancient Sparta that includes information on the cult of Artemis Orthia.

Chrimes, K M T. Ancient Sparta: A Re-Examination of the Evidence. 1949. Manchester, Great Britain: Manchester University Press, 1999.

A fascinating albeit somewhat rare text that primarily explores evidence from the temple of Artemis Orthia at Sparta. It is a dry, academic text, but the information presented within is fascinating.

Clark, Gillian. Women in Late Antiquity: Pagan and Christian Lifestyles. 1993. Oxford: Oxford University Press, 1994.

A good text about women's roles in ancient Greece and Rome that can help anyone understand the roles of women and Goddesses in ancient Greek religion.

Cole, Susan Guettel. Landscapes, Gender, and Ritual Space: The Ancient Greek Experience. Berkeley, Los Angeles, London: University of California Press, 2004.

An invaluable text for anyone wanting to learn about Artemis. This book contains an entire section that discusses Artemis and some of Her various functions. It is especially valuable for women wanting to find particularly feminine ways of honoring Artemis.

Condos, Theony, ed. Star Myths of the Greeks and Romans: A Sourcebook. Grand Rapids, Michigan: Phanes Press, 1997.

This fabulous text contains a translation of Catasterismi *by Pseudo-Eartosthenes and* Poetic Astronomy *by Hyginus. This books is particularly valuable because I know of no other English translation of* Catasterismi, *and it contains some particularly interesting versions of the ancient astronomical myths. I originally tracked down this book to discover if the myth that Artemis once loved Orion was actually true, or if it was just a modern invention. I discovered that it occurs only (as far as I know) in Poetic Astronomy, which is a Latin source that deals with Diana and the Roman pantheon. I have not been able to find it in any Greek source, so it seems to be a version of the myth that is particular to Diana and may not apply to Artemis.*

Connelly, Joan Breton. Portrait of a Priestess: Women and Ritual in Ancient Greece. Princeton, New Jersey: Princeton University Press, 2007.

An excellent book with a wealth of information on all types of ancient Greek clergy. It is equally valuable to men and women, and includes some interesting information about Artemis and the women who served and honored Her.

Deacy, Susan and Karen F Pierce, eds. Rape in Antiquity: Sexual Violence in the Greek and Roman Worlds. 1997. London: The Classical Press of Wales, 2002.

An excellent book for helping modern people understand ancient Greek concepts of sex and sexuality. Aside from aiding and understanding of Artemis's virginity, this book can also help people comprehend Persephone's marriage to Hades and what significance that might have held to ancient people.

D'Este, Sortia. Artemis: Virgin Goddess of the Sun & Moon. London: Avalonia, 2005.

While I find the title of this book to be misleading at best, it is still a good reference text. D'Este presents many, many myths and epithets and titles of Artemis and, most importantly, cites her sources for each of them. While I would certainly not use it as a guide to Artemis, it can be an extremely useful roadmap for people wishing to track down ancient sources. I should mention, however, that her pronunciation guide for the various epithets of Artemis is based on modern Greek, not ancient Greek, so it does not actually give readers an accurate idea of how the ancient Greeks would have pronounced Artemis's titles.

Downing, Christine. The Goddess: Mythological Images of the Feminine. 1981. New York: The Crossroad Publishing Company, 1989.

While I certainly don't agree with every little thing in this book, it does give a wonderful modern perspective on Artemis that I find generally fits with my experiences with Her. It's worth looking at for anyone who specifically wants to approach Artemis with a modern point of view.

Guthrie, W K C. The Greeks And Their Gods. 1950. Boston: Beacon Press, 1955.

A nice, if somewhat old fashioned, introduction to the Greek pantheon.

Hope, Murray. Practical Greek Magic: A Complete Manual of a Unique Magical System Based on the Classical Legends of Ancient Greece. Wellingborough, Northamptonshire: The Aquarian Press, 1985.

This book is an invaluable gem for people creating any sort of modern spirituality involving the Gods of ancient Greece. While it is now out of print, used copies are not terribly hard to find. This book contains incredible insight on how to create or discover your own personal spiritual path involving the figures of ancient Greek mythology. I highly recommend it to anyone who has a personal relationship with any ancient Greek deity.

Kerenyi, C. The Gods of the Greeks. 1951. London: Thames & Hudson, 2000.

While I am not a huge fan of Kerenyi, many people enjoy his books. He gives a decent overview of ancient Greek mythology, but he does not make much of distinction between Greek and Roman sources, and at times does not cite sources at all. For some this is not a problem, but I think it can be somewhat misleading in places.

Kramer, Ross Shepard, ed. Women's Religions in the Greco-Roman World: A Sourcebook. New York: Oxford University Press, 2004.

A good collection of information on women's religious practices, including some references to Artemisian cults.

Larson, Jennifer. Greek Nymphs: Myth, Cult, Lore. New York: Oxford University Press, 2001.

An excellent book about ancient Greek nymphs that also contains a section specifically examining the nymphs in relation to Artemis.

Lefkowitz, Mary. Greek Gods, Human Lives: What We Can Learn From Myths. New Haven and London: Yale University Press, 2003.

An excellent book for helping modern people understand how the ancient Greeks conceived of Gods and mortals as fundamentally different beings, and what impact that had on ancient Greek religion and theology.

Lefkowitz, Mary R. Women in Greek Myth. Baltimore, Maryland: The Johns Hopkins University Press, 1986.

A fascinating book about the roles of women in ancient Greek myth, including women who were involved with or servants of Artemis.

Melas, Evi, ed. Temples and Sanctuaries of Ancient Greece: A Companion Guide. Trans. Maxwell Brownjohn. London: Thames and Hudson, 1973.

This book contains fascinating chapters on the sanctuaries of Artemis at Brauron and Sparta, as well as chapters about many other prominent ancient Greek temples and sanctuaries. It is worth reading for its perspective on Greek religion as directly related to the sites in which it was practiced.

Otto, Walter F. The Homeric Gods: The Spiritual Significance of Greek Religion. Trans. Moses Hadas. 1954. London: Thames and Hudson, 1979.

While this book is written in prose, it speaks like poetry. It eloquently describes the essence of the ancient Greek Gods and can help anyone understand the beauty and divinity beneath the ancient myths.

Parke, H W. Festivals of the Athenians. 1977. Ithaca, New York: Cornell University Press, 1986.

A comprehensive book about ancient Athenian festivals, including festivals of Artemis. Anyone at all interested in the ancient Athenian calendar ought to read this text.

Pomeroy, Sarah B. Goddesses, Whores, Wives, and Slaves: Women in Classical Antiquity. 1975. New York: Schocken Books, 1995.

A good overview on the lives of women in ancient Greece and Rome.

Pomeroy, Sarah B. Spartan Women. New York: Oxford University Press, 2002.

A fantastic book about the roles of women in ancient Sparta, including information on how they partook in the cult of Artemis Orthia, and what we can learn about them because of that.

Rice, David G and John E Stambaugh, eds. Sources for the Study of Greek Religion. Number 14, Society of Biblical Literature: Sources for Biblical Study, ed. Burke O Long. Scholar Press, 1979.

This book provides various primary sources concerning different aspects of ancient Greek religion. It also includes many commentaries from ancient scholiasts, which are otherwise quite difficult to find. It includes information on worship of Artemis as well as other deities, and would be incredibly valuable to any Helleniste.

Schwab, Gustav. Gods and Heroes of Ancient Greece. Trans. Olga Marx and Ernst Morwitz. 1946. New York: Random House, 2001.

I mention this book only because it is exceedingly rare that I come across a modern retelling of the ancient myths that I actually like. Schwab presents the Greek myths in a way that reads like a novel, yet is true to the ancient sources. For people looking for a book that presents the ancient Greek myths as a single continuous story, this is the one to get.

Simon, Erica. Festivals of Attica: An Archaeological Commentary. Madison, Wisconsin: The University of Wisconsin Press, 1983.

Another excellent text about the ancient Athenian festivals. Simon covers what Parke did not, and adds information that was not yet available when Parke was writing. In particular she presents a wealth of information on the Arkteia festival, which Parke does not mention.

Sissa, Giulia. Greek Virginity. Trans. Arthur Goldhammer. Cambridge, Massachusetts; London: Harvard University Press, 1990.

This book is invaluably important for anyone who wants to understand why Artemis would have manifested to the ancient Greeks as a virgin, what significance Her virginity had to Her ancient worshippers, and what significance it might have today. Sissa presents a wealth of evidence that explores the paradox of ancient Greek virginity, and eventually explains some of its underlying beliefs and concepts. Anyone, reconstructionist or not, who works with any of the ancient Greek virgin Goddesses ought to read this book.

Spawforth, Tony. The Complete Greek Temples. London: Thames and Hudson, 2006.

A good book about the architecture and use of ancient Greek temples. To my disappointment, it covers only colonnaded temples, and thus excludes the temple of Artemis Orthia at Sparta. Even so, it does present information about many other temples of Artemis, as well as information about various aspects of Greek temple worship. It would be very helpful to any Helleniste wishing to create their own sacred space dedicated to any ancient Greek deity.

Vernant, Jean-Pierre. Mortals and Immortals: Collected Essays. Ed. Froma I Zeitlin. 1991. Princeton, New Jersey: Princeton University Press, 1992.

A fabulous collection of incredibly insightful essays. Vernant includes a number of essays about Artemis, particularly focusing on Her liminal aspects. The information he presents and the insights he gives make this book a valuable resource.

Von Rudloff, Robert. Hekate in Ancient Greek Religion. Victoria, British Columbia: Horned Owl Publishing, 1999.

An excellent book about Hekate that also includes a healthy section about the similarities and differences between Her and Artemis. Rudloff explains where, when, and how Artemis and Hekate converge and diverge.

Winter, Sarah Kate Istra. Kharis: Hellenic Polytheism Explored. Cafepress.com, 2004.

My hope is that this excellent book will replace Old Stones, New Temples and become the common guide to Hellenismos. It is a fantastic introduction that helps beginners grasp the concepts behind Hellenic practices.

Zadiman, Louise Bruit and Pauline Schmitt Pantel. Religion in the Ancient Greek City. Trans. Paul Cartledge. Cambridge: Cambridge University Press, 1992.

A good overview of urban Greek religion. It includes little tidbits about Artemis here and there, but generally focuses on Greek religion as a whole.

Some Recommended Primary Sources

I list these particular sources because they are some of those that I know of that can be useful to people studying Artemis. They are by no means the only valuable ancient sources, nor is this necessarily a comprehensive list of all sources relevant to Artemis. Some of these sources include references to Artemis that are relatively obscure, whereas Artemis features centrally in others. I encourage readers to enjoy the process of hunting down references in ancient sources, and to relish the thrill of discovery you get when you find something you've been looking for.

Aeschylus: *Agamemnon*
Suppliant Women

Apollodoros: *The Library of Greek Mythology*,
also known as *Library and Epitome*

Aristophanes: *Lysistrata*

Aristotle: *Athenian Constitution*

Bacchylides: *Odes*

Callimachus: *Hymns*

Diodorus: *Library*

Euripides: *Hippolytos*
Iphigenia in Aulis
Iphigenia in Tauris
The Suppliants

Herodotus: *The Histories*

Hesiod: *Theogony*
Works and Days

Homer: *Illiad*
Odyssey

Pausanias: *Description of Greece*

Pindar: *Odes*

Pliny the Elder: *The Natural History*

Plutarch: *Aristeides*
Themistocles
Theseus

Pseudo-Hesiod: *Homeric Hymns*

Xenophon: *Agesilaus*
Anabasis
On Hunting

About the Author

Thista Minai began independently studying various forms of Neo-Paganism in 1996. She began to consciously strengthen her lifelong relationship with Artemis in 1999. She found her calling in Hellenic reconstructionism in 2004, and founded the Temple of Artemis at Cataleos in 2005. In 2006 she became an *exegete* of Artemis in the organization *Neokoroi*, and in 2007 became the director of the *exegetai* program. For more information on *Neokoroi*, go to:

http://www.neokoroi.org/

43909703R00089

Made in the USA
San Bernardino, CA
01 January 2017